DIGITAL MARKETING *for* Professionals

*How To **Attract** and **Retain** Your Ideal Clients*

NICK BAGGA
(THE SME STRATEGIST)

The digital age has brought with it a whole new breed of business person. And Nick is certainly a prime example of a modern day success story. The epitome of an entrepreneur, he's one of my elite coaching members, mentee and a personal friend. His passion for educating others makes me delighted to engage him to run monthly workshops at The Internet Business School. It's this same drive that led him to write *Digital Marketing for Professionals*.

The book covers all the major strategies, tools and techniques that encompass digital marketing, with subjects such as how to run internet campaigns, optimise websites and make the most of social media. There is also invaluable information on using Google Ads, SEO and Google My Business. Each subject is broken down into digestible bites, making it a breeze to understand.

The value of the book is that it teaches the very same know-how Nick delivers when consulting with his clients. He has a unique ability to take complex tasks and simplify them, one of the reasons he's so sought after in his field of expertise. The book takes you on a journey that builds knowledge, each chapter focusing on a specific area of online marketing. The exercises and explanations provide a clear guide to communicating an engaging digital message unique to the needs of your business, and which resonates with potential clients.

There is no quick overnight fix, but through practising these creative digital marketing techniques, and some trial and error, you too can build a sustainable lucrative business.

Simon Coulson (Managing Director, The Internet Business School)

I have worked closely with Nick for some time now. He's a valuable resource and advises our firm on digital marketing strategies and implementation. Nick is a trusted partner when it comes to making the online presence of our business distinct and effective, bringing us the clients we want for our tax and accountancy practice and specialist wealth management products. With a focus on connecting to SMEs which fits our target market, his marketing strategies are aligned with our goals.

For the business professional it is important to be told not what you want to hear, but what you need to hear. Nick does just that, and this is evidenced in his book. It explains not just the tools and techniques for digital marketing, but the rationale behind them. As a professional advisor myself this straight-forward advice is well appreciated. For any expert selling their services in their chosen field these insights make it easier to recognise the purpose behind the processes of digital marketing, all of which the book details in a clear fashion.

This book makes the reader stop and think about their goals, and how these relate to bespoke methods of online promotion. There are exercises to get you started and recommendations given for all the major platforms and sites where a business can market its services. For anyone looking to implement expert digital marketing strategies that engage with their ideal client this is an excellent resource. The book delivers a great return on investment and is one I'm happy to recommend.

Andy Turner (Associate Partner, Devonshire Green)

ISBN: 978-1-9161651-3-7

First published 2019

Disclaimer

CONTENTS

PREFACE

A quick Google search reveals a ton of information on the subject of digital marketing. So why do you need my take on it? In short, why choose this book?

To fully understand the answer, I guess it's first necessary to appreciate my 'lightbulb' moment. This came seven years into my career as a chartered accountant. (Yes, that was my previous life.) Well paid, successful and at the top of my game, my position as a financial and business analyst for large FTSE 250 corporations meant I should've been happily sailing into the lucrative future shining before me.

But… I was dissatisfied. I'd lost interest in this kind of work. Dare I even say, I was bored?

The bombshell of an in-house restructure gave me the nudge (shove!) I needed. The time was now or never, and instead of being shocked by a situation out of my control, I actively embraced redundancy. What an opportunity to steer my career in a new direction and take on a new challenge.

I was lucky. Over the years my natural flair for marketing had been noticed. Colleagues would often question why I wasn't working in this field. Being someone who has always enjoyed networking and building new relationships, I had to agree. Without even realising it, my financial career had given me many transferable skills. I would often have to liaise with and consult key clients – mainly SMEs in professional services across the UK – to advise companies on technological changes and software solutions. This often meant interacting with the sales and marketing teams, and so the seeds of my interest and passion were stirred.

My personal path to marketing expertise

I took the time to consider my next steps. Personal development was key. The first few months after leaving the financial world were spent figuring out how I could best leverage my skills, not to mention attending just about every marketing event on offer. What followed was a considerable investment of time and money into further education, and it was during a high-level marketing course that I became aware of my true purpose. My future would be spent mastering the best digital marketing strategies available, both to grow my own company and to help SME owners improve their online marketing.

Starting out with only a minimal marketing budget gave me the raw edge necessary to successfully employ these strategies. I honed and pruned a number of effective techniques and key tactics to drive targeted leads. This was both fascinating and deeply satisfying, I learned powerful methods to draw ideal clients to select my expertise over others in the marketplace. Bear in mind I was doing this working from my home office and spending a fraction of the typical costs of a big advertising campaign, showing just what can be attained with the right approach. The results were beyond my wildest imagination, achieved within an incredibly short timeframe.

This experience was invaluable, and my client base grew. I adopted and fine-tuned certain methods, soon succeeding in winning over important contracts. As the months rolled by, this process snowballed. CEOs, directors, SME owners and other professionals started recognising what I was doing, including some previous contacts from my corporate days. Existing clients recommended me to their colleagues and peers, and my digital marketing company continued to grow.

I quickly came to realise it's not that people are unwilling to make positive changes and embrace digital transformation, but to do so they need to understand just how powerful digital marketing really is. Once they learn what's available and, most importantly, recognise they don't need to spend enormous amounts on advertising, it becomes easier to accept, indeed welcome, cutting edge marketing methods.

Why *Digital Marketing for Professionals*?

Quite simply, it's because digital marketing is a world of mystery to many. Sure, there's a multitude of tools out there, as well as various texts on the subject. But they all have one thing in common: they're complicated. *Way* too complicated.

From my individual consultations, client experiences and workshops it became obvious there was a real need to break down this confusion. There was a gaping hole in the market for a digital marketing book that genuinely addressed this issue, keeping it simple, and providing a clear strategy for utilising the power of digital marketing to help grow any business of any size.

And so the idea for *Digital Marketing for Professionals* was born. This book is the fruit of my experience and aims to help you build a better version of your business online in the same way I have.

Demystifying the world of digital marketing

The book offers you a unique opportunity to learn more about the many facets of marketing available, and what digital strategies and tactics you can employ to give you the edge over your competitors. But, most importantly, it removes the shroud of mystery that overwhelms many when they approach the subject of digital marketing. Even if you hire someone to carry out your marketing for you, it's still a wise choice to be informed about what digital marketing is. That way you can explore the possibilities and options available to maximise your earning potential.

In essence, this book provides you with the step-by-step information necessary to truly understand why your business needs to embrace digital marketing, as well as the tools and methods necessary to successfully wield this powerful instrument to transform your business, and ultimately, your profits.

NICK BAGGA

INTRODUCTION

The enigma that is digital marketing

I regularly consult with many business owners, sales professionals and top-level executives who tell me they don't understand what digital marketing is, or how social media campaigns can help them grow. You probably feel the same way.

While I can teach you about digital marketing and the available tools, that's just the start. In addition, you need to know *what* they are, *why* they work and, most importantly, *how* they can be implemented. In fact, the confusion surrounding the subject often means professionals frequently give up and return to their comfort zone of the same old marketing methods they've been applying for years.

In a world with an ever-increasing digital footprint, ignoring digital marketing is professional suicide. In today's fast-paced society where we're bombarded with more information every minute, knowing how to get your message out there is crucial. This book will give you a solid grounding in the digital marketplace so you can understand it from the bottom up.

A unique way to connect directly with your clients

It used to be that businesses could rely on word of mouth referrals to generate regular revenue. Those days are long gone, as savvy modern consumers turn to the internet to compare businesses to find the right one to provide them with solutions. If they don't find you there, as far as they're concerned, there's a problem.

While some professional sectors are traditional in their approach to marketing, forward-thinking, pro-active firms are forging ahead, taking advantage of the new way of doing business to generate leads and profits at an unheard-of rate. If you're not one of them, you'll be left far behind. Today the ability to compete for new clients is not limited by geographic location. However, it can be restricted by a lack of presence in those places where prospects are searching for help.

It's more important than ever to ensure high visibility, offer greater value and present a proactive solution to potential clients' problems. Relationships are key, with trust and reputation being built in a very different way. Digital marketing allows you to reach out and connect directly with a client on a personalised level. While this is hugely beneficial, it takes time to build a brand and generate awareness, especially since clients are increasingly selective and suspicious of hard sell techniques.

You need to engage with prospective clients in the online places they occupy and show them what you can do for them.

Digital marketing need not be confusing or needlessly complicated

In fact, it can be just the opposite. *Digital Marketing for Professionals* doesn't simply provide you with the very best tools and principles necessary to successfully grasp the subject. It takes the process one step further. The book breaks down individual marketing strategies and techniques into their *what, why* and *how*. This means you'll learn *what* a tool does, *why* you need it and *how* it benefits you. There are many advantages to following this KISS (Keep It Super Simple) approach, not least of which is that it provides a fast-track method to truly understand how each one works and how to put it in place correctly.

This book is an easy-to-digest, practical guide written in straightforward language to help you make the most of your business. It applies equally to new start-ups and long-established professional firms. The information you'll learn as you work through its pages will lead you down the path of becoming more marketing savvy, and teach you how to identify and attract your ideal client.

Who is this book for?

While there is much written about digital marketing, a large proportion of this focuses on selling more products to consumers. That is *not* covered here. Instead, this book deals with offering professional expertise to business clients and forging mutually successful relationships. It's for anyone who provides a service to SMEs based on acquired knowledge, skill and experience in a given field.

Those who'll benefit from this book include:

- Professional service firms (accountants, lawyers, consulting firms)
- Architects, interior designers, property developers, surveyors
- Financial planners and advisors
- B2B providers
- C-level executives
- Sales professionals
- Professional coaches and consultants
- Thought leaders or emerging authorities
- Any professional with a new start-up
- Anyone looking to generate leads for their business

How To Use This Book

The book follows a clear structure, each chapter starting with a brief introduction and ending with a takeaway section for your reference. Together, they help you understand the process of marketing your business, supported with simple exercises so you can put what you've learned into practice straight away. Although it's been written so the reader progresses steadily through the various marketing tools covered, it's also possible to jump straight to any particular one of interest and benefit from it.

The first few chapters discuss the importance of understanding your ideal client and how to identify your target audience. They also explain how to define your business goals and choose the right marketing campaigns. Chapters four to twelve delve deep into their subject matter, covering a wide range of powerful techniques, including leveraging LinkedIn, getting set up on Google My Business and maximising the use of social media. As you follow the detailed steps and guidelines throughout the book you'll be establishing a solid online presence, as well as learning little-known secrets about digital marketing.

What you will learn

For simplicity, and in light of my background, I've placed an emphasis on accounting firms throughout the book. For those working in a different type of professional service the content is still wholly relevant to you. All my techniques are transferable and highly applicable to modern marketing.

Within the pages I'll cover:

- How to optimise your website properly
- How to create a professional business blog
- How to make use of paid search advertising
- How to benefit from search engine optimisation
- How to set up Google My Business and manage your reviews
- How to obtain, engage and convert leads through LinkedIn
- How to use other social media: Facebook, YouTube, Instagram and Twitter
- How to get the most out of email campaigns, webinars, podcasts and events
- How to measure your key performance indicators accurately and use metrics

Once you've worked through the first few chapters and established your core knowledge, you'll then advance through the key marketing strategies, tools and techniques.

Digital Marketing for Professionals gives your business the edge over your competitors

As you see results, you'll have gained the confidence to decide what works best for you. This brings with it the competitive edge necessary to draw in the right clientele and, as you advance, the skills to successfully explore and take advantage of the many other options out there.

Digital Marketing for Professionals shares my knowledge and experience. I've included relevant case studies and exercises that combine to ensure your message speaks to your target audience. From best practice ideas for enhancing personal branding to tips and tricks tailored towards growing long-term visibility and authority, this book will enable you to take control of your online presence and make it central to all your marketing. In addition, I'll suggest some awesome tools you can put to work straight away to begin your journey.

Are you ready for digital marketing success? Let's get started!

CHAPTER 1

DIGITAL TRANSFORMATION: DIGITAL SELLING FOR TODAY'S MODERN BUYER

Business and commerce are huge driving forces in our professional and personal lives. Since the development of the internet and its mainstream usage, how we go about building and advertising our businesses has changed quite radically.

Thanks to the development of social media, we now have a marketing tool in our hands which is more powerful than any we've ever had before. Today, we have the means to address and speak to the 'ideal client' directly, online.

The combination of commerce with communication via social media has created the trendy terms of 'Digital Selling' and 'Social Selling' but while they may seem jargonistic, their relevance to any business enterprise cannot be ignored.

Technology has transformed our entire world. Nowadays, connectivity is simply different to any other age in human history. We can communicate with people across continents just as quickly and easily as we can to those living next door. The pace of change brought about by fast and direct communication through the internet means it's imperative that a business adapts and takes advantage of new channels of marketing, or risks being left behind by its competition.

What is Digital Selling?

Digital selling is, in effect, a different entity from social selling. You may have heard of social selling previously, so what is digital selling?

The term 'digital selling' is quite a compelling one, as it's a broader term which encompasses social selling. Essentially, the concept of digital selling is all about using the power of the Web and Social Media to sell our services, goods and products. Digital selling involves leveraging digital assets to generate leads and nurture prospects to move them closer towards the sale. It includes things like sales automation, digital documentation and online presentations.

Social selling on the other hand is simply one element of digital selling. In a nutshell, it's when sales people use social media platforms and specific tools within the digital space, such as LinkedIn Sales Navigator, to interact directly with their target audience. Ultimately, the goal is to gain valuable consumer insights and build trust to eventually achieve a sale.

The digital age has seen a huge movement around the way in which professionals need to sell their services. In the past there was a significant amount of trust placed in the reputation and name of any professional advisor. If you were looking for one, say an accountant or lawyer, you may have found there was only one choice in your local area.

That professional could dictate terms, meaning they could determine the price. The lack of an available alternative meant, for the most part, individuals would have to take it or leave it with regards to hiring their services. Clients could only hope this person gave them good advice and looked after their best interests.

In the modern world, this is no longer the case. In fact, competition has risen to levels we could never have previously anticipated. Today, we can easily find a range of accountants to pick from, even in a small town. Competition has become far more pronounced. More significantly though, so has the means by which you, the professional, can become visible to potential clients.

The Traditional Ways

In the past, you'd find your advertising and marketing would match the size of your business. Trying to outsell a competitor who was already well known would have been a challenge. Why would someone risk using a 'new business', when they could use the tried and tested local option?

In the past, businesses would often use marketing methods such as:

- **Cold Calling.** An act where you would call numbers in your geographical location, hoping someone might need your products or services.
- **Cold Mailing.** From direct-mailing an entire community to sending emails to anyone on a contact list, cold mailing was also very popular.
- **Qualifying Leads.** A qualified lead is someone who could be a legitimate target for your business, but you do need to first ascertain their validity.
- **Classified Ads.** From the *Yellow Pages*, which had its final run in January 2019, to local newsagents, classified ads were a common resource to try and search for customers or clients based on their needs and location.

As you can imagine, old school marketing solutions like this were slow, cumbersome and not quite as likely to work. They were broadly managed and would use a 'hit and hope' kind of system to find a potential client. By making enough calls and spending a lot of time mailing and delivering, you could eventually gain some new sales.

The digital era has changed this entirely. Budgetary constraints no longer stop a business from being able to promote itself using a website or social media platform.

A New Era of Opportunity

While not 'easy' by any means, a business owner can start up a new business and have a hugely professional, experienced and trustworthy looking online presence created in the space of a week.

This means that, with more competition today, the 'ruling' firms of the past no longer have it quite so easy. Thanks to the rise of digital marketing such limitations are no longer so prevalent.

Today you are not restricted quite so significantly by your starting out position as a newcomer. The digital era has allowed for new kinds of businesses to rise and the days of needing elite level expertise and decades of experience to build a new business are long gone.

Through digital marketing, it becomes easier for businesses to get themselves spotted. If you make the most of the tools used by the digital marketing industry today, you can help your business to outgrow the constraints you might have faced in the past.

Of course, it's not as simple as merely deciding that you want to promote your services and gain new clients from marketing. If you want to get the best from different marketing opportunities, you need to first understand what options exist for your business.

In the past, a business had to try and cater itself to everyone. If your advertisements were going to be seen by the entire public, it was better to try and pander the message to fit with a particular way of thinking. But this is in the process of immense change. The digital marketing era now means that **instead of targeting everyone**, you need to **target someone specific**.

The power of digital marketing means we can adapt the message to fit to a more well-defined persona, based on what can be gleaned from analysing habits and trends of interaction by internet users. However, it does mean prospective clients now expect adverts to jump out at them and be tailored to their own interests and message.

This is, typically, where problems tend to begin for the average business owner. You could find it hard to work out who your 'ideal' client would be. You may also find it tough to come up with a clear plan as to what kind of message would fit your target market the most. Gaining expertise in digital marketing will allow you to better understand how to identify and attract your ideal client and strengthen your online message.

This should give you an immense appetite for making the most of digital marketing. Used correctly, it might just be the single most important tool you have in your arsenal. **It enables your marketing to be more specific than ever and better target potential clients, allowing your business to really pinpoint the individuals who matter and make any promotional communications more direct.**

The art of digital selling changes everything. Instead of simply trying to find a problem that someone in your local area might have so you can give them a solution, you must offer something more. Rather than merely seeing your business as a solution provider to those who come across it, consider that digital marketing allows you to achieve the following:

- Cultivate a whole new list of people interested in your expertise.
- Target individuals who are a natural fit for your products or services.
- Provide value and empower interested parties through education.
- Demonstrate to people that your business is more than just a point of sale.
- Develop the role of a trusted authority figure in your industry.
- Share the human side of your business through insights.

Now, you might presume that digital marketing is going to die out. You might even presume that how or where you operate is too 'small' for digital marketing to be relevant for your business. However, keep this in mind: by the end of 2020, around 70% of the world's populace will have access to the internet via smart devices.

At present, there are 4.3 billion internet users worldwide, of whom almost *65%*, equating to more than 2.5 billion users, are estimated to be online via a mobile device, according to Internet World Stats and Statista.

This changes everything really.

Individuals can be targeted by businesses today on a live and active billboard they routinely carry around in their pockets. This is the power of digital marketing. You aren't just looking to catch the perfect client when they are on a lunch break, or when they're walking down the high street. Now, you can target specific groups of people based on everything from their question selections on a search engine, to their social media statistics and personal details.

In the past, businesses might have had an average or good idea of who their ideal client would be, but found it difficult to reach out to them directly. Effective digital selling requires you to have a clear list of profiles, identifying those individuals who would make the perfect clients for you, and where you can connect with them online. This is powered by the growth of social media.

Today, we can find out metrics and information about someone that we never would have thought possible. These include; age, location, gender, occupation, and interests.

Everything is now out there to be found, analysed and used to help build your client profile. With marketing solutions which now allow us to target people in a way that was never possible in the past, there is no real need for wide-net marketing. Even traditional advertising methods, such as newspaper ads and billboards, need to be re-designed and tailored to fit a certain message.

Digital marketing offers the easiest possible solution to that problem. Now, your business can proudly proclaim itself as an expert in its field, with solutions aimed at solving a particular groups' problems. For example, an accounting firm with construction industry expertise can now create a campaign which speaks directly to local builders and tradesmen.

Previously, an accounting firm would have had to try and tailor their message to anyone and everyone who might have needed help with their accounts. Now, the same firm can run a series of campaigns, changing the message to fit to different characteristics of their target audience. The immense rise of competition and choice in every sector of industry, in every part of the world, means you no longer need to target everyone and hope for your message to reach a potential client. Instead, individuals actively seek out a business which speaks directly to them.

Prospects are put off by catch-all business advertisements. They want to feel like a business is personally speaking to them. Instead of looking to help everyone solve one problem, you want to help a specific group of people solve many related issues. Your firm should build its success around a core group of clients who regularly look for your advice knowing that you understand the unique challenges they face. These challenges can be because of their specific industry and any rules or regulations governing it, the markets they operate in or another distinctive feature of their trade.

Digital marketing enables you to align your strategy to address these issues, unconcerned that it won't interest other prospects. In this way you ensure more of your clients are a natural fit for the solutions you provide. Your campaigns are designed around the idea that you could well be the best professional available to solve those issues of a particular nature.

The emphasis is on creating the marketing content to speak to a distinct target group, which means you have to do **less general chasing**, and instead work out ***who*** **would be worth chasing** in the first place.

Rather than cold calling every potential client in a wide audience, digital selling enables you to entice, attract and eventually **bring these individuals to you**. You could be using your website to do this, or you could set up social media campaigns and/or implement email marketing.

You may even choose to offer value in the form of a digital event like a Q&A session or a webinar. This is where the immense scale and potential of digital marketing really comes into its own.

Social media is such a strong tool of opportunity, as it enables you to target the right people, at the right time. With users bombarded by more potential business offers than ever before, accuracy is key. You will simply get lost in the maelstrom of offers and deals out there if you are not an exact fit for your client.

The Modern Buyer

It would be wise for any business in the modern world to use social media to help them better target potential new business. The old ways of having to either address everyone via broad advertisement or cold calling are gone. So are the days of having to target entire industries and niches.

How someone chooses a product today versus how they did so in the past could not be any more different. For example, modern buyers are far more likely to be influenced outside of their social circle. In the past you would often use a friend or family member to recommend your services initially to potential clients.

Now? This is no longer necessarily the case. Prospects will listen to expert opinions online; they will turn to reputed online sources and look to social media for information. This has become the norm and is a massive part of the buyer's journey. It means that the modern buyer has more opinions to consider, as well as more choice.

The internet and the era of digital marketing give you the opportunity to be far more specific in your communications and the targeting of them. If you cannot do this it becomes much harder to land the perfect client.

Social media makes it easier to define clear categories for everything in an industry. It's all about engaging with people online, giving them something of value in return for their interest in your business. You are encouraged to share value with your client base, answering questions of all kinds and advise with relevant information. **Giving out something for nothing on social media can reap long term rewards.**

When you provide your prospects and clients with answers and reference guides which they can absorb and refer back to when needed, they appreciate your input in their business. This was not something that was considered before, when clients had little choice over who to select as an advisor in their local area. Today however, the sheer scale of opportunity created by digital marketing has brought this to an end. Clients can now pick and choose who they work with to ensure they receive good value, which is why **you need to promote your worth and skill set.**

So, as you can see, the modern marketing industry is aeons away from the business world of the last century, or even the last decade. **How then, can you find out who your ideal clients are? And more critical for your long-term success, how can you target them via digital marketing?**

CHAPTER 2

HOW TO IDENTIFY AND ATTRACT YOUR IDEAL CLIENTS

In the last chapter I mentioned the dramatic shifts taking place within the world of commerce. There has been a total switch in the way we try to seek out new clients, build networks and develop our businesses. For firms in the professional services industry, these differences have become more pronounced than ever before.

Hopefully, you now recognise that the internet gives professionals more opportunities to find and target clients, and how old-school methods are no longer quite so prevalent. Times change, as does business, and the practices we use to secure the future of our businesses have changed too. Through the art of digital selling, we've seen a major transformation in the ways you can connect to potential clients and how to convince them **you are the expert or firm** they should be listening to.

However, the hard part you may have now is identifying the **ideal client** for your business. Let's look at some of the things you need to consider as you start to build a picture of your ideal client persona.

As mentioned, targeting the right people is more possible than ever. Doing this through digital channels can allow the content to be much more aligned and compelling to your defined prospects. How then, can you make sure your digital marketing strategy is designed so that your communications reach this select audience?

Identifying Your Ideal Clients

The first process you need to undertake to create a modern and successful marketing campaign is drawing up a profile of your ideal client. Determining and refining this picture to work out who your ideal client is takes a huge amount of time, effort and energy. If establishing a successful business is your long-term aim, you need to be ready to identify who your ideal client would be.

Most professionals get caught up looking only into the more outwardly defined attributes such as the industry type, but you should also work out **who they are**, what kind of **role they operate** within and the **reason they would need your help** in the first place.

For professional service providers, your ideal client would most likely be someone who you can work with on a long-term basis. As a professional, you are reliant on repeat business from your clients and want to see them engage your services regularly.

For any business of this kind, it's important you consider the use of the **Pareto Principle**. This principle states that around 80% of your business will stem from just 20% of your clientele. This is shown to be applicable in many service industries, especially those offering professional expertise. This indicates a business which may be growing all the time, but still maintains a regular stream of clients who trust and value what is on offer.

If you want to try and determine what kind of clients you should be including in your top 20%, then consider the following:

- What kind of industries are you most aligned with and suited to helping?
- What is the rough business size or sales volume of your ideal client?
- How much, approximately, would you expect these top 20% clients to pay you?

- What is the geographic spread or main location of your ideal client, as you may need to visit or meet with them?
- What are the challenges they may face that are peculiar to their operations or business model?
- Who will be your point of contact? Are they a key decision maker?

Once you can answer these questions, you are ready to take positive steps forward. Naturally, as time goes on, you'll want to add more clients that match to this top 20%. Who should you be looking for? That's entirely down to how you answered the questions above.

At this stage, I'd recommend trying to create what I call your Ideal Client Profile (ICP). This should include details about the business such as:

- The number of years the business has been running and the number of employees.
- A turnover that is within your understanding but offers potential.
- A location and an industry placing which have opportunities for expansion and scaling up.
- A business with ambition at the top and decision makers who are open to change.
- Currently profitable but could potentially improve its margins.
- Where the managers are willing to make investments in their business and play by the rules.
- Are happy to pay for quality services and don't always decide on the cheapest option.

Of course, this all comes down to what your business is built on and your own long-term goals. Nobody can define this for you, it's your vision and aspiration which guides you on ***who* and *what* you wish to target.**

For example, you could easily find yourself targeting as far and wide as construction companies, property management firms, exporters, car parts manufacturers, charities or government bodies. As an accountant, or some other kind of professional for that matter, you are lucky in that you will be able to target many business owners, company directors and senior executives (every enterprise needs to manage their tax, legal, IT and compliance affairs after all).

You will always need to provide a range of services and have a satisfactorily broad client base to ensure a steady flow of work, but some tasks and clients will demand more time dedicated to them than others. Not all clients will be interested in the add-on services that require a higher level of expertise or knowledge of rules and regulations which you may have.

However, with that in mind, you need to know what forms the core services of your firm and where you want to position yourself in the market. Not every accountancy firm is suited to audit international businesses but, equally, those that do this won't draw in clients who are small family ones. You could have a more specialised level of appeal such as wealth management or forensic accounting so it's vital you target the right people with that in mind. **You want to get as many high-paying clients as you can, who let you use your time wisely.**

So, having considered all of the above your ideal client would be:

- A business which needs your help on a monthly or annual basis.
- Someone who is willing to work with you, leveraging your expertise to achieve new goals.
- A professional who needs help with those activities you specialise in handling.
- Companies or organisations who operate within the sectors, fields, industries or markets you know best.

For different businesses and types of professionals, you can see how it can be both simple and challenging to find your ideal client. The scope of some professions such as accountancy or law is so wide, it can feel like both a blessing and a curse to businesses trying to choose the right expert. How can your firm work towards locating these prospects who would match to your profile? How do you spot someone needing worthwhile professional expertise on a regular basis to someone who would see you as an administrative assistant?

EXERCISE

Using the ideal client profile criteria, make a list of 5-10 companies, or individuals, that would make ideal clients for you and your firm.

Identifying Your Ideal Client In-house

The starting point for many firms when it comes to categorising their ideal client would be to look at their current clients. The best resource here is your own previous experience, so look at the clients you already have on your books: which of these do you enjoy working with the most and which provide the most reward?

The clients who give you the greatest intellectual challenge and responsibility, alongside the highest and most consistent financial return, will be your ideal clients. Instead of trying to paint a picture of a business owner or executive in your head, let previous clientele do the painting for you.

Simply look at what you are currently doing, who you are working with, and how they help you to build your business. You then need to start shifting your search and your hunt to businesses more akin to these positive clients. **The biggest challenge you may face when identifying an ideal client is learning to say no to negative clients.**

In a bid to get any business, you might just take on those menial, financially unrewarding jobs. At the start, that's fair enough: every accountant or other professional must build a reputation. When you want to become more specialised though, you must learn to refuse clients that aren't close to your ideal. If you don't, they'll refer you to other people from their side of the business, making it more likely you attract less suitable clients. I like to refer to these clients as 'leech clients', the ones that drain your time and resources for very little in return. Be sure to let go of any 'leech clients', you'll be much better off!

NICK'S TIPS

If you're a new start-up firm, start building your ideal client profile (ICP) from Day 1. This is exactly what I did and it has served me well. You really want to start attracting quality clients from the get-go. It's better to reduce your prices for those first few ideal clients if you need to, than take on clients you don't really want to but feel you have to. This will definitely help your business grow by bringing in the right people, at the right time and at the right price.

Using the Power of Social Media to Identify Your Ideal Client

While you can find out much about what your business can and cannot do by referring to its previous successes and failures, other solutions also exist. Social media makes it easy for you to research, qualify and identify those truly desirable clients. Of all the social media platforms, LinkedIn is the best source of information for that purpose.

LinkedIn is the social media platform of choice for professionals. Using it enables you to get much more specific business information on potential clients than you could from their Facebook, Twitter and/or Instagram accounts. It's very informative and will likely go some way to helping you identify how ideal a fit they would be. From LinkedIn you can identify the senior management of any organisation, looking at everything from the size of their business to the profile details they provide about themselves, learning a lot in a short space of time.

You should make sure you regularly network through LinkedIn, as it is such a powerful platform for B2B service providers. It can deliver so many valuable connections and leads. Since you are able to learn so much about prospects' professional and personal expertise, you will then easily determine how well aligned they are to your long-term goals. The more you do to establish the suitability of a prospect at an early stage, the better.

By the same token, a useful tool to turn to for analysis is Google Reviews. Simply look at the kind of reviews that potential clients are getting, as well as those they are leaving. Are they leaving feedback on other businesses? How often do their own clients comment and review the work they do?

Reading into the comments of their own clients can provide you with a unique insight into their business relationships too. Doing this gives you a better idea of who they are, what kind of services they offer and what kind of benefits you might receive from working with them. For example, you maybe notice people talking about delays in their work or a lack of efficiency. What could you do to help them change that process? Perhaps there's a cash flow issue you could help them resolve on a regular basis?

It's all about looking for the little clues that indicate whether a potential client might turn into a valuable long-term business ally, as much as it's about learning to avoid low-potential clientele.

Lastly, I recommend you spend some time checking out online forums. In terms of getting insight into a potential client, forums tend to give you a good idea of how engaged they are with their own customer base. You want to work with passionate professionals who realise their business goals, as they are more likely to see the value in the full range of services which you offer.

Working with clients who are happy to just coast is likely to produce less than stellar results. Instead, target those who are ambitious and engaged themselves. You are looking for long-term relationships with clients and shared growth and development.

This is all well and good, but how do you find ideal clients outside of this?

Finding Your Ideal Clients

Now that you know how to consider a prospect and determine how well they would fit simply by using your own experiences and social media tools to get a closer insight, what is your next step?

Locating those leads who fit your ideal client profile is also about determining where they have an online presence through which you can connect. For any accountant you will likely find LinkedIn, as I mentioned previously, is a great starting point. Here you are able to research your ideal client, simply by using its diverse range of search features to track them down.

You need to read into the personality as well as the professional background of any lead. That's why I'd recommend using additional tools such as Facebook for a bit of personal analysis. This allows you to take a much closer look at the individual and their interests so you can find common ground.

One reason you should pay attention to the person behind the business is because you want to know they are passionate and driven. Those who are not forward-thinking might not take your services as seriously as you would like and be more inclined to see your accountancy expertise, outside of the basics, as a needless expense.

Nobody likes it when their efforts are not properly appreciated so you only want to work with those individuals who can see the value you bring and are prepared to act on your recommendations. Using social media such as Facebook, and especially LinkedIn, you can start to validate those really good leads based on the tells and information prospects present about themselves on their profiles.

Once you are armed with this kind of information, I'd recommend you start looking to use social media to drive any interaction with your business. It's easy enough to do this: you simply need to ensure you start using the same platforms as your ideal client.

By the same token, your firm's website and social media should be redesigned and enhanced so they reflect the specialist skills, vision and solutions you provide and what you are all about. This helps to draw in your ideal client by making the message resonate with them, suggesting you would be the right choice to fit their needs.

Remember that cost comes into any decision on who to engage as well. Sometimes it's better to take the client who offers a lower initial fee but is better aligned to your business and long-term goals, than to take on an unsuitable but high-paying client. While an engagement might not seem so profitable at the outset, it could lead to more in the future, with other services upsold on the back of a preliminary contract, or through referrals.

Still unsure about how to use social media for lead generation? Don't worry, I'll go into this in more detail later. For now, though, let's pay attention to making sure you can attract your ideal clients appropriately.

Attracting Your Ideal Clients

To truly grow your firm in the digital age, you need to be ready to build up a strong online presence. Sure, referrals are great, but they can't always bring you the ideal client. And when they do, that ideal client will want to know all about your business. This means your firm must have a great website and social media pages, channels and materials which all give the right impression and reflect you in the best possible light.

If you are serious about attracting your ideal client, then you first need to make sure you work towards building a high-quality informative digital identity. This should showcase the best qualities of you and your business, highlighting what makes you distinct from all the rest. **The world is loaded with accountants, all targeting fellow professionals, so what makes you different, exactly?**

It's important you make yourself stand out with one or two specialist areas of expertise. For example, if you are specifically looking to target those in the IT sector, it will be much easier to attract them if you showcase additional skills or knowledge based around this particular industry.

It's better to have a more specialist style as:

a) it makes you more suitable to your ideal client and,

b) you can charge more thanks to your added skill and specialism.

There are many ways to attract new clients to your business. You could run online marketing campaigns to bring them to you; find them on social media and make a direct introduction; meet them through a networking event, at a trade show or similar; or you could even be introduced to them in a social setting.

For many professionals, geographic location may not be an issue when considering who you can work for, though for others it may be a barrier. When drawing your ideal client to you using online marketing, you should mix this in with third party referrals or good, sound networking expertise. If your aspirations include establishing the firm as an international leader in its chosen field, then you will look to break through any online or real-world restrictions to sourcing good prospects.

It's vital you post bespoke content for your ideal clients, written specifically to attract and target them. Ensure you post this content through the right channels, where your ideal clients appear to spend most of their time interacting and building their networks, and don't forget about following media sites and pages which could be relevant to them. Getting the content structured correctly can be a little tough, but I'll go into that in more detail in Chapter 5.

Do You Understand Your Ideal Client?

The most critical thing though, is to **fully understand your ideal client's goals and ambitions**. Again, you are not looking to simply perform some function or set up a process, you are looking to add value to a client's operations. You should aim to find long-term clients who can really benefit from using your expertise. To do so, you need to work out what is holding your ideal client back, and what potential obstacles could be in their way to achieving their goals.

Then, you build all your communications and marketing around showcasing yourself as *the expert* to solve their problem. Your ideal client will be attracted to the fact that your marketing, delivered directly via social media or otherwise, speaks to the issues they face. The content should make them recognise that you have considered their position and have made it clear you are perfectly aligned to helping them. They should see your marketing and think; *'This is the expert who will advise me on how to take my business to the next level!'*

That's crucial. Clients will be attracted to a firm that can see the obstacles in their path and help to clear it. **More importantly, ideal clients will be attracted to a business which stands out from the crowd.**

Your business absolutely must stand out for all the right reasons. It should be shown as more than a bog-standard accountancy firm. Look at what your online and offline marketing materials say: do they make you stand out to your ideal client?

You know the possible problem and perhaps even the solution, for what your ideal client needs. Do you come across as the expert your potential client is looking to engage with?

Take the time to rebuild all your marketing material to be shaped around this kind of thinking. The more specific it is to the problems of your ideal client, the more likely they will be attracted to the services you provide.

Every good business has a 'Why'. You need to be ready to show the world your story, and make sure this reads like the perfect solution to your ideal client. How do you go about creating that business message? How do you define your goals to ensure they tally up with your ideal client?

Takeaways

- The world of business has changed immeasurably, you have to be prepared to act and adjust to match up.
- This means constructing a profile of your ideal client, which includes doing a lot of research of your own.
- You should auto-analyse your business and work out where changes need to be made to align with your ideal client's requirements.
- You must understand your ideal client, their goals and concerns, using social media tools like Facebook and LinkedIn to work out their professional and personal style.
- You need to be able to attract clients using the right tools, positioning your firm as the solution to their problems and the one that can help them to succeed in their aims and ambitions.
- Lastly, you have to present a clear story. You must show your ideal client what makes you better than the potential competition. This means speaking to the client directly and showing them you offer the solution that resolves their immediate problem, as well as expertise which can help them avoid possible future ones.

CHAPTER 3

DEFINING YOUR BUSINESS GOALS AND CHOOSING THE RIGHT MARKETING CAMPAIGN

In Chapter 2 you learned how to create an image of your ideal client. For your business to be a success, it must know *who* it will target, *where* it will target them and *how*. This is clearly one of the most pivotal parts of running a successful business, especially for a professional services firm. You have a lot to consider as an accountant, as some clients will be more useful to you than others. The ability to target more rewarding clients is always going to be a long-term benefit to your business.

Now, let's take a closer look at choosing the right marketing campaign to do this. It's not only about attracting the attention of those who will rely on your professional expertise. Running a good quality marketing campaign comes down to what business goals you want to focus on and meet as the outcome of it. Thus, it's crucial to understand and be clear on what your objectives are before diving into setting up a marketing campaign.

The broad nature of digital marketing means that working out what kind of campaign you wish to run can be challenging to say the least. When you know what your desired outcome is, and you are clear on your short and long-term goals, you'll be able to direct your energy into the right marketing campaign and employ the right tactics. This ensures you really make the most of your time and budget. It will help to cut down on wasted opportunities and generate maximum impact with every promotional communication.

This chapter will help you to better understand:

a) what a marketing campaign is and,

b) how to pick the right campaign for your exact needs.

While the desire to bring in more leads is an obvious one for your firm, I'll help you to more adequately align your business offerings with the needs of your ideal client to achieve this.

Let's start by looking at how you can clearly define your business goals. If you do this, you'll be much better prepared to position yourself to stand out from the crowd.

Defining Your Key Business Goals

Before jumping in and deciding what kind of campaigns you should run, it's important you take the time to identify what you are looking to achieve. Your business and marketing must understand its objectives at a level that can be distinct and measured for. Simply having lots of clients and turning a profit is nowhere near detailed enough.

Instead, you must be very specific indeed about the kind of business goals you wish to put into place. The easiest way to do this, of course, is to determine what kind of professional you wish to be. From an accountancy perspective, you could have expertise in a particular industry or area of tax. You may wish to help IT contractors in the private sector for example, in which case you would build your business goals around IT contractor accounting specialising in IR35. Alternatively, you may wish to concentrate on offering advice in research and development tax credits.

You should always look to offer a specialist service which justifies using *your* business over the competition. This would mean building the whole business message around it. **Nowadays, it's not enough to simply say you want to generate leads, make sales or keep your clients. What do you stand for? Why do you want to run a particular campaign style?**

Before you start up that Facebook or LinkedIn marketing campaign, or begin contacting local businesses, let's look at some key things to consider. Your ideal marketing strategy should be designed to carry out some, or all, of the following goals and processes:

- **Solving problems.** The first aim of any marketing campaign is to introduce yourself as the solution to a given client's problem. Whether you do this by looking to find those already aware of their problem, or by raising awareness of said problem, is entirely dependent on the campaign.

- **Show the solution.** By the same token, every campaign should be styled to flag up to the individual the solution they will receive from you. Think of the before shot of a frustrated business owner, and the after shot of someone running a profitable business which performs to expectation, as a good example.

- **Encourage repeat business.** Your marketing campaigns should also be built around making sure your previous clients come back for more. For an accountant, this could be built around themed marketing to do with specific dates and deadlines, encouraging them to act.

- **Continue upselling.** You also want to make sure every project, and each campaign you run, shows your existing clients what else you can do for them. From introducing new services to seasonal offerings, each campaign should aim to get existing clients investing in the additional services you offer.

- **Deliver on expectation.** Each new client targeted should be your ideal client, and since they are your ideal client, you may have to go above and beyond the norm to reach them. This means your campaigns should look to deliver a reputational boost, creating value-driven messages that indicate to potential clients you are able to live up to your promises.

Of course, not every marketing campaign will need to cover all these goals, but somewhere down the line you should have marketing campaigns which do aim to do all the above. Trying to both retain clients and introduce new clients to your business all through the one campaign can be tough. As an accountant, you may find it easier to run different campaigns for different kinds of markets, depending on what you are trying to achieve from them.

EXERCISE 1

Make a list of your short-term and long-term business goals. Are you *absolutely clear* on what it is your firm wants to achieve? If yes, then great. If not, spend some time defining your business goals before you start thinking about what marketing campaign to run.

What Campaign Should You Run?

With the above in mind, it's important to remember that you need to choose the right campaign style. Certain messages work better with certain kinds of campaigns. You should look to run not just one all-reaching campaign, but a particular *kind of* campaign.

Before continuing, it's essential to recognise what is meant here when talking about running a marketing campaign. Most of the time, a campaign is seen as something quite short-term: over within a short space of time. Yet a marketing campaign can run for just a single day or for a decade. There is no guaranteed half-life of a marketing campaign and with enough incremental changes, you could run the same marketing campaign for years!

Naturally, there are numerous choices to consider. When you are trying to target those ideal clients, you tend to have three options to pick from. Most campaigns fall into one of three categories: **Attainment, Monetisation** and **Interaction**. If you want to run a great campaign for your accountancy firm, then understanding their differences is vital to selecting the one you need to fit your objectives.

Let's look at what each of the three categories could mean for you. Each one is very specific and differs from the others. Crucially, each of these campaigns will be used to help achieve at least one of the goals previously mentioned.

Attainment Campaigns

The first kind of marketing campaign often suggested to you would be an Attainment campaign. This kind of campaign is designed around making sure you can attain, or acquire, new prospects and clients. It's an appropriate strategy for those who wish to make an impression in a new area, within a new industry, or simply wish to expand upon their present client base.

This is what people mean when they say they wish to run an Attainment campaign: they want to acquire more leads and/or clients. The style of this campaign is usually built around using promotions and social media strategies to help show people you:

a) understand their problem and,

b) can solve it in a way that's easy for the client to grasp.

If your marketing goal is to reach out to those facing a problem you have the skills to solve, or on addressing potential clients in a specific field which matches your expertise, then you need to run an Attainment campaign.

The reason this style of campaign is successful is that it draws individuals to you who might have either been unaware or uninformed about what you have to say. It's aimed at capturing their attention and making them aware of both the problem and the solution.

How an Attainment campaign works is quite different to other campaigns, as it cannot really be judged using profit as a marker. While you will convert your leads into sales eventually, it's more about attaining new leads and increasing awareness of your services. It's all about making that initial connection to individuals who at some point may wish to hire you. The nurturing of any prospects or leads to move them further along the buyer's journey and marketing funnel are follow-up activities of this campaign.

One way you could run an Attainment campaign, is to target it towards specific services. For example, if your accountancy firm offers wealth management services, you could look to advertise these as openly as possible. It's a valuable service, but often one that is hard to promote too blatantly. If you wish to advertise it, the ideal time would be during an Attainment campaign, by introducing the service and making it known widely to prospects who are unaware of how it can benefit them.

Attainment campaigns are often very particular as they are all about turning someone from an unaware or uninterested person to a prospect and then into a solid lead, who may later become a client.

For one of my clients, an accounting firm in Essex, my team set up an Attainment campaign for them to advertise their specialist property tax planning services, using LinkedIn. That campaign drew in circa 300 new leads within the first six weeks. In fact, my client landed a major real estate company in London off the back of it with an ROI of 750%. My client later told me the real estate company they landed had been searching for a specialist property tax firm for a while.

The consistent content we were pushing out for the firm resonated with the managing director of the real estate company, who got in touch with my client through LinkedIn. This is a great example of how specialist services are needed out there, people just need to be made aware of them and constantly reminded of where to find them. This is the power of social media campaigns, when they are implemented correctly.

Monetisation Campaigns

The next kind of campaign you may wish to spend a bit more time learning about is a Monetisation campaign. Such campaigns are all about leveraging your present client base and making them more valuable to you. It's also about monetising those leads you acquired with your Attainment campaign.

From pushing new services you have introduced, to encouraging more conservative clients to be a bit more ambitious by taking up extra services, these campaigns come in many shapes and sizes. The goal here, unlike for Attainment campaigns, *is* to make a profit. It's about converting those leads and existing clients into profitable sales and encouraging higher take up on your full range of services.

Of course, building a Monetisation campaign would be needless for those accountancy firms who are just starting out. The goal of this kind of campaign is to help turn the leads and clients *you already have* into more profitable ones. If you have no clients to begin with, naturally you won't benefit from this category anywhere near as much.

This is the right kind of campaign to implement when you wish to bring in more revenue to increase your bottom line, by maximising the potential of every existing lead and client. The objective can be measured in sales conversions.

A good example is one which specifically promotes a more specialist service you offer. An accountancy firm could draw attention to wealth management services in both Attainment and Monetisation campaigns, as this is a very popular add on service many clients will wish to benefit from.

The secondary aim of a Monetisation campaign is to get your existing clients to spend more with you on exclusive, specific services. This could be useful for promoting things like private workshops for company directors advising them about their legal duties. You could charge a select number of your clients a quarterly membership fee, entitling them to come along to private events where they'll benefit from expert advice in specific fields not readily available elsewhere. The more premium services you can convince someone to invest in the more successful your campaign will be.

Interaction Campaigns

Interaction campaigns are instead built around creating brand loyalty and client dependency. For an accountant, this means designing a campaign that is positive, optimistic and makes your services seem more widely accessible.

It's all about creating new business through leveraging your client base. This can include creating brand advocates to help promote your firm, brand and vision.

Not every business can afford to have an in-house promotion team. As an accountant, you are often unable to make the hard sell that some other industries could via Interaction campaigns. Instead, you want to match this up with your brand story: what makes your accountancy practice so unique?

You can then make this uniqueness your focus in any Interaction campaign. Create lots of valuable online content, offering advice and insights which other accountants would expect to be paid for. Show your story as a business and tell people more about why you are an accountant worth using. It's much easier to sell your story as a benevolent professional when you are happy to give out useful advice. This helps you to gain greater visibility too, being seen as an expert who is not always prioritising payment for every service rendered.

The return on investment you receive from this is long-term loyalty from clients. You make them more likely to share your name with fellow professionals and to speak of you positively to others. Giving away information that people would normally expect to pay for might instinctively seem like bad business sense, but it really isn't if it's done the right way.

You could then have existing clients become brand promotors using your best clients to recommend your business. This could be done using testimonials and client stories. They'd be able to help advocate your quality as a business and recommend your services as a professional to friends and other business contacts. They could also be used to help actively promote your business; doing this through blog posts, online videos and social media content to help spread the word about the quality of the services which you provide.

Picking the Right Campaign for Your Firm

Of course, you now need to decide what the right campaign is for the stage of your business growth. I recommend that as time goes on, you try and use a mixture of all three campaign styles. It's vital you do this, as each campaign will play a role in securing client loyalty, building your business brand *and* helping you to locate more of your ideal clients.

By using a considered mix of all three campaign categories, you make it much more likely to achieve all the five goals mentioned earlier, among others. Each strategy will help to retain existing clients and attract new clients, who use more of your services. Meanwhile they will all actively promote your business name, brand and expertise as time goes on.

Generally, try and consider the following ideas:

- If you are just beginning to build up your professional firm and currently have no real clients to speak of, or want to raise awareness of the business to acquire new leads, then you need to start with an **Attainment campaign**.

- If you already have some leads and existing clients and you simply wish to make sure they recognise and take advantage of your range of services, then you should run a **Monetisation campaign.**

- When you have a list of regular clients who are using your services, then you should look to run an **Interaction campaign** to help them feel encouraged to promote you elsewhere.

Starting with this information, you will be able to grow towards creating a more holistic marketing message. Once you know **what** to target, **who** to target, and **how** to target you can make your campaigns much more effective.

As this book goes on, we'll look more closely at some of the most pertinent and notable marketing strategies around, which can only be of benefit to you long-term.

EXERCISE 2

From your identified business goals in Exercise 1, now try and work out which marketing campaign would be most suited to your goals, based on your own needs and the kind of clients you wish to target.

Now that you understand the essential points of creating a strong and holistic marketing message across all your campaigns, let's look at making your firm appear as attractive as possible to your ideal client. To do so, you need to put in place some fundamental changes to your business website to ensure you stand out.

Takeaways

- Every good professional firm has a clearly defined series of business goals, identifiable by the various select or specialist services they promote.
- Each campaign that you run will be different, with distinct targets and objectives, ensuring they are fit for their purpose.
- Determining the right kind of campaign (Attainment, Monetisation or Interaction) for each marketing need and current stage of your business development is essential.
- You will be much more successful if you understand **what**, **why** and **when** to use each kind of campaign, depending on your aims.
- Picking the right campaign allows for better results and avoids your marketing from feeling too generic and universal.

CHAPTER 4

WEBSITE OPTIMISATION

In the last few chapters, you've taken the first steps towards building a strong foundation for your business. You've learned the importance of creating your ideal client profile and put in place a clear plan of how to attract these clients to your business. Now, you need to go about making your business appear as the perfect choice to sign up that ideal client. To start with, you should ensure you have a quality website.

As we move forward now, we're going to look closer at the nitty gritty of marketing. You'll pick up some very important things to do and some key strategies to grow your business sustainably for the future.

But before we move any further forward and delve into the specifics, you must first get your own house in order, which I like to refer to as *'laying the foundations'.* For your firm to be able to stand on its own two feet, it needs to have a strong, stable base. You wouldn't move into a house that doesn't have a solid, secure foundation; having a quality company website is no different.

Let's face it though, if you don't have an optimised website, compelling content, relevant functionality and a strong Call-to-Action, you are leaving a lot of potential business on the table.

What is Web Optimisation?

The term 'web optimisation' or 'website optimisation' can be considered to mean a lot of different things. Typically, web optimisation is the process used to enhance the performance, visibility and relatability of your website to ensure it delivers for your long-term business goals.

Some tend to refer to web optimisation as conversion rate optimisation, for the simple reason that it helps your business turn more visitors into buyers by converting prospects into sales. Whether your goals are to help reduce rejections or improve sales, you'll find that optimising your website to suit your business needs is key to making those goals possible.

There are many things which will come up with regards to revolutionising and rebuilding your website. There are some things that you need to fully understand with regards to what has to be built into the website's content and functionality. For example, are you aware of the different forms of website optimisation?

You have two forms: onsite and offsite. I'll cover this in more detail as the book goes on but, basically, onsite optimisation revolves around making changes to the website itself. It can also be known as Onpage and Onsite SEO, which is the practice of optimising elements within a website. This looks at what can be done to improve the content's relevance to a search engine query. It's things you can do internally on your website, whether it's optimising your page content by using specific keywords or optimising your images by using the 'alt' tags.

Offsite optimisation on the other hand is about making changes to other sources of marketing, such as social media and paid advertising, to help drive more traffic to your website using external links. I'll cover this later in Chapter 7. For now, though, you should look at putting into practice six major tactics that will help your business to start moving away from its present predicament, encouraging your website to attract new prospects and, thus, swelling your income.

Why do You Need an Optimised Website?

Website optimisation matters primarily because your website must be successful in the eyes of its users. Everyone who comes along to your website is looking for you to answer a question, a query, or to help them find a solution or complete a task of some capacity.

Put simply, the aim of website optimisation is to bring you more conversions, sales and clients. If you were to run an ecommerce website, for example, you would be optimising it to increase the number of people who visit and **actually buy something.** For your accountancy firm, it would be about increasing the number of people who visit your website that **contact you** or **initiate the sales process.**

This can be done by using various forms of optimisation and a lot of A/B testing or split testing. A/B testing is running two different campaigns which say different messages but try to produce the same end goal. Whichever one proves to be the most successful should then be retained, with the other dropped or modified.

When your website is optimised, it naturally becomes a more effective tool for you and its visitors. An optimised site draws more traffic, enhancing your visibility, improving the likelihood of prospects and leads finding it. The website should take your prospect on a journey, from finding it to engaging and connecting to your firm through it, and in time, converting visitors into becoming clients.

For your accountancy firm, you will need to optimise your website, tailoring it to draw in your ideal client. Whatever issues or ambitions they have; your job is to design its content to sound like *the place* to find said information.

Your site literally becomes more useful to your business activities if you optimise it. It's like producing a flyer but forgetting to include a contact telephone number or email address. You would never produce marketing material with obvious mistakes, so why do so with your website, one of your most valuable lead generation tools?

However, remember that your website is not merely for converting leads into clients. It's also about generating new leads. If your website can bring in a healthy combination of both new leads and higher conversions, it's doing its job.

How Can You Optimise Your Website?

Now obviously, improving your website to produce more leads is something every business wants to do. Who wants less leads, or less revenue? Nobody!

There is however, a lot more to optimising a website than simply throwing in a few links and adding in a few keywords. While the adage of *build it and they will come* is very much true here, you need to construct something credible in the first place. Take a strategic approach to your website, looking at both page design and content optimisation, as this allows it to do a more effective job of promoting your services.

But first, before we start looking at the different tactics that can be used to optimise your website, it's important to gain an understanding of the lead generation process. As generating leads is one of the main goals of website optimisation, it makes perfect sense to understand the process of how a casual website visitor or prospect turns into a lead. Check out Fig. 4.1 below which shows the general components at play in the lead generation process.

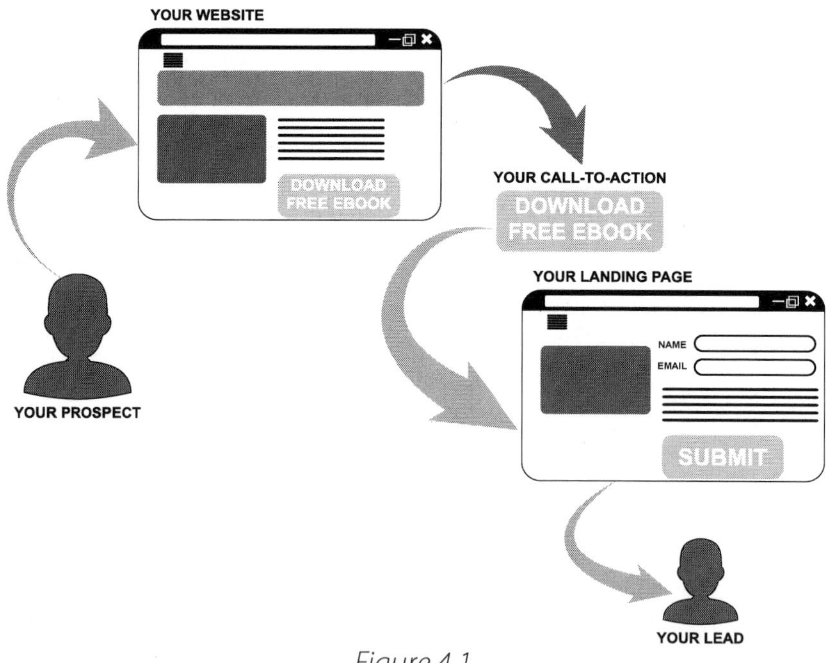

Figure 4.1

The lead generation process typically starts when a user clicks on one of your Call-to-Action buttons, located on one of your site pages or blog posts. The Call-to-Action *'Download Free ebook,'* as seen above, leads the user to a landing page where they'll be asked to provide contact details so that you can get in touch with them. Usually, this means getting a name, email address and/or phone number for site visitors. This is the most vital part, as the landing page enables you to capture their details turning them into leads.

Remember, the Call-to-Action in our example above doesn't have to be a free ebook, it can be a free report, article, whitepaper or anything else of value. Whatever you think your ideal client could benefit from receiving, you can offer as part of your Call-to-Action. The essential component in this process is the landing page used to capture leads. Think of it like a fishing net, where you are trying to grab as many leads as possible, drawing them in with something of interest, the bait.

The overall lead generation process will be explained in more detail later in the book. For now, it's important to note that the key foundations for successful lead generation begin with a Call-to-Action.

There are lots of key points to consider to help build up website traffic and engagement. Here is a list of ways you could add content, to improve or otherwise change up and increase the quality of your firm's website:

- Adding in new forms to your most regularly visited pages. From long-read blog posts to FAQs, inserting contact or comment forms on these to generate interest and to inspire interaction makes a lot of sense.
- Using analytical tools to identify which parts of your website are most effective and those that are not engaging visitors to the standard you want or expect.
- Creating relative links across your site from page to page, where there is a valid reason for inserting the link. Advertising and linking

must *always* be relevant to the actual content in question. It should also include an appropriate Call-to-Action to make the most of the link, encouraging clicks which can result in conversions.

- Offering added value via free ebooks etc. loaded with information you would normally charge for, or available as part of another consultation. The downloadable offer should take the user to a landing page, as mentioned earlier, asking them for a name and email address to receive their item, netting you a hot lead to follow-up on.

Choosing the Right Website Platform

Of course, running a website takes a lot of work. Like any structure for your business, virtual or otherwise, it needs strong, secure foundations. To return to the housing analogy from earlier: you wouldn't buy a house that was built on quicksand, would you? Likewise, you want your website development platform to be a solid bedrock that supports your entire digital presence.

Many 'DIY' systems such as Squarespace, Weebly and Wix offer useful solutions for some businesses. There are numerous website design, development and content management systems out there to choose from. To make things simple, we're going to look at the most popular types of DIY website platforms with a quick overview of what they do.

Drag and drop Website Builders (best for beginners)

Website builders such as Wix and Weebly are geared up to making life easy for beginners or those that just want a quick and simple, uncomplicated website. There is very little or no scope for changing the pre-set design templates. This can limit functionality but means you can put together a website in less than an hour.

Another advantage of these more standard website builders are the simple pricing plans. There's usually a very basic free option, but if you want some professional features such as a domain name and ad-removal you simply pay a set monthly fee with no optional add-ons.

Fairly Flexible Website Platforms (best for intermediate users)

Squarespace and Webflow are good examples of website platforms that are slightly more complicated and boast more features than the beginner ones.

Squarespace is a popular option that allows more design freedom than drag and drop builders but isn't as flexible as the more advanced platforms. However, Squarespace is ideal for easily creating ecommerce stores and offers great support with fast-response 24/7 live chat.

Customisable Website Platforms (best for advanced users)

Platforms such as WordPress allow a high degree of design freedom and adaptability but can be more difficult to use due to the advanced features. Other flexible platforms such as Magento are specifically aimed at e-commerce and offer features geared up to building digital storefronts.

These websites will need a fair bit of technical know-how as they are not as intuitive to use. Having said that, there are some page builder themes and plugins which WordPress offers that allow you to customise every component on your site without writing a single line of code. You can hire specialists that will do the work for you but this will add considerably to the cost.

Also, be aware that WordPress comes in two forms:

- wordpress.org - the full version with a huge range of plugins and integration
- wordpress.com – a watered down version of WordPress that is restrictive, but easier to use.

Deciding on a Platform

The reason to choose a specific platform is straightforward. You need to make the building of your professional website as easy as possible. What works for you will be dependent on the size of your firm, your long-term goals and the stage of development you are at.

There are some pretty standout choices. Whichever one you decide to go for, be sure to consider the complete functionality of the system. You could find choosing the wrong platform may leave you hindered when it comes to adding more advanced or bespoke features which have the potential to take your business to the next level.

Let's compare a couple of options: WordPress and Squarespace.

WordPress Versus Squarespace

- With WordPress, you have unlimited control over all your pages. You can make them look as you wish, choose how you want them to flow and have as many as you desire. With Squarespace, designing pages is easier *but* there are fewer options in terms of quantity and display.
- Squarespace will host your website for you which means you can get started quickly and easily. On the other hand, you have to host your own website with WordPress, giving you total control over everything that it can do for you.
- WordPress has a steeper learning curve due to the sheer power it offers, but it has limitless potential. Alternatively, Squarespace is simpler and easier to manage. These things are important to consider, allowing you to expand your website content and marketing tools as you set new objectives for them.
- The same is true for the design element. Squarespace is initially easier to use, with a host of free designs available, but they do have restrictions on how they can be adjusted. WordPress has many paid

and free themes you can opt for, including more customisation possibilities, allowing you to adjust your website exactly as you see fit.

- Squarespace allows you to build a slick, professional website very quickly (within a couple of hours) and everything is included in a set monthly fee, including hosting. This makes it a convenient option if you are pressed for time.
- In terms of adding advanced features to your website, WordPress has many standard ones but can be made much more impressive with the use of plugins and the like. With Squarespace, you are limited to the built-in templates which may be enough for you, especially as they are very well-designed.

This is just a quick analysis of the differences between WordPress and Squarespace. To sum it up, Squarespace is great for a quick, simple solution that isn't too difficult to use. WordPress is a better selection if you prefer more design freedom, advanced features and you don't mind investing time and effort in building the perfect website.

If you're still not sure, I'd recommend you start by looking at WordPress. It's among the most powerful around and makes it simple for you to build a website that can be scaled, adjusted, edited and improved as time goes on.

Certain platforms might make creating a website seem easier on day one, but there's a chance you will eventually outgrow them. While WordPress might seem more confusing to use than some of the others mentioned above, once you get past the learning curve, it responds well. It's easy to control and offers you more possibilities, either for yourself or your development team, to make advanced improvements.

It's probably also worth mentioning that WordPress can be hugely advantageous when it comes to added SEO benefits, which will be explained further in Chapter 7. As WordPress is open source, it's much easier to add to and completely adjust your site. Also, this makes it simpler to optimise images to be more SEO-friendly, alongside using useful and well-respected plugins such as All in One and Yoast SEO. These points all centre around ways to get your website moving up the search engine rankings.

A client of mine, an accounting firm based in Surrey, previously used Squarespace as their content management system. I advised a switch over to WordPress after reviewing their content and business objectives. After the migration, we found their blog posts performing much better on Google, generating far more traffic. One particular blog post we wrote for them, on helping contractors decide whether to set up a Limited Company or operate through a PAYE umbrella, jumped up 12 places to rank on the first page of Google in just a few weeks, whereas it previously ranked on the second page. Google loves well-optimised content, so why make life complicated? Embrace what works. WordPress makes it easier to please Google's algorithms, which will reward your business.

Having said that, there are legitimate reasons to opt for Squarespace. If you are severely limited on time, you're perfectly happy with the pre-set designs on offer and you're not too worried about maximising SEO results, then Squarespace is a viable alternative.

The important thing is to weigh up the immediate pros and cons, but also think long term, i.e. how you want your website to be in a year or several years' time. Built with the right foundations, there's no reason why your website cannot become a major part of your marketing strategy for years to come.

Six Major Tactics of an Optimised Website

Of course, regardless of what platform you select to build your website on, the content should be well presented and informative, the site must also be easy to navigate. To help you optimise your website, I have laid out some fundamental tactics you should look to employ if you want to make the right impression. There are so many different ways and means of making a website more optimised, but the ones below are central to increasing relevant traffic and generating leads. Each tactic will play a key role in the development and growth of your business, so it's essential you include the six below if you want to make sure your firm's website ranks high in the search engines and stands out from the competition.

Have a Strong Headline & Call-to-Action

The first tactic of including a strong headline and Call-to-Action should include four essential components which I like to refer to as *'the shopfront'* or *'merchandise window'.* The presentation must draw the visitor in and aim to keep them on your website for as long as possible. The first thing you must do then, is to ascertain what the pain points of your prospects are. The pain point, typically, would be something that they could identify with as a major issue in their business. Pain points can vary in terms of their level, usually on a scale of 1-10, with 10 being the highest. The more significant the issue, or the bigger the barrier to their success, the more important it is to do something about it. You can offer a way to interrupt that pain by entering into the conversation going on inside their head.

The best way to help describe this is using the AIDA (Attention, Interest, Desire, Action) principle. AIDA is not only a famous opera, it's a process that you can use to turn a casual observer into being someone who is totally committed to your vision. This principle helps to grab the attention of a visitor to your website and turns them into an interested party, one who can fully see the benefits you provide. How do you do that? Let me show you.

The first thing you need to do is grab the reader's attention by hooking them in with a punchy headline. **ATTENTION** is the first part of the AIDA principle. You bring their attention to the problem they face, and you let them know you empathise and appreciate the issue at hand. For example, small business owners could be concerned that their accountant is always too busy to talk to them on the phone, seldom available, or even worse, doesn't return their phone calls. What your website needs to do then, is address this issue with an attention-grabbing headline. You could say something like:

"Are you tired and frustrated of waiting around to have an important call with your accountant, so that you can make those really critical and time sensitive business decisions?"

The subheading could then be something like:

"We understand how it feels to be undervalued and that's why our firm is proud to guarantee a call back to all enquiries within 24 hours"

Hopefully, you can see how the above demonstrates a good example of a headline that presses on the prospect's pain points to then get them ready to engage with your website.

I just did a random search for an accounting firm in a random location in Greater London and this is what I found on their homepage:

"We offer specialist tax planning and accountancy services to small and medium sized businesses. Our commitment is to get to know each one of our clients and help them reach their business goals."

It then goes on to talk about the firm and how long they have been in business. Not a single mention of 'you', the potential client, and what 'your' problem might be. There are so many websites like this that aren't bad websites, they simply do not focus on the potential client and what their problems might be. What you must do then, is put yourself in the mindset of the reader, rather than focusing on yourself. You should be thinking with the *WIIFM (What's in it for me?)* attitude, but from the prospect's perspective. As a general rule of thumb, you ought to look for a ratio of two 'yous' and yours' for each one 'we', 'I', 'us' or 'our', etc.

Similarly, let's look at the two following headlines:

"Effective tax planning for small business owners"

"Are you looking for a larger tax rebate? Did you know you can reduce your tax bill by up to 70%?"

Both headlines cover the same topic within the article, but which of them do you think is more appealing to visitors? Which one would *you* click on? One tells you something that you already know. The other opens your eyes to how much the expert can help. I know who I'd go for!

The second part of the principle is **INTEREST**. Now that you've hopefully managed to get the reader's attention, you then need to start building up their interest in the solution you can bring them. Statistics show that you only have 3-5 seconds to capture the interest of your prospect before they are gone, possibly forever. So, in the example above, the subheading here would be an example of the interest created. It could also be something like:

> *"Get the help that you deserve starting today – a fast response from committed professionals!"*

Naturally, this creates an immediate interest in the offer that you provide. You have informed the reader you care and resonate with their problem.

Now that you have caught their interest and they are intrigued; you can move on to the next part: **DESIRE**. To awaken that desire, you must be ready to start working towards moving the prospect over the line to become a client. This means you need to offer something which your competition isn't. For example, you could include a free report or article on your website for users to download called *'The top 5 things to consider when choosing an Accountant'.* Before the article download, prospects would have to enter their name and email address in the box provided. At this point you would now have their details and as long as they have consented to receiving further information, which they should agree to as you have, hopefully, earned their trust, you are in a position to provide further advice via email. The email content then helps to push your prospect further along the line to buy from you. This is known as a drip campaign.

Only 3-4% of your prospective buyers are ready to make a purchase or a decision to get in touch immediately from your website. Therefore, by continuing to provide value to your prospects by giving out useful information via email in drips, they'll be much more likely to buy from you once you have generated some goodwill.

Now that you have some leads who are very much interested and can see what you are able to do for them, it's time to move to the final phase: **ACTION**. This is when you implement that Call-to-Action: making it clear how the prospect can get in touch with you. Something as simple as:

> *"Call one of our friendly team members now on {NUMBER} to set up your free, no obligation consultation."*

Alternatively, if you want them to leave their details for you to call them back, then simply direct them to a form for this on your website by displaying a clear link to the page where they can leave their contact details. Be sure to finish the job and 'close the deal', or else all your marketing efforts here would have been for nothing.

Remember, your marketing plan must portray your firm as the obvious choice, making it a no brainer for prospects to buy from you.

Deliver a High Conversion Landing Page

The second tactic to improve your website is to **create a high conversion landing page**. As explained above, a landing page is essentially where individuals are directed to by your marketing efforts. The goal for an effective landing page is to get the user to take action. It's an essential part of any sound marketing strategy. Whether it's a free ebook or article you're offering, your sole aim is to capture the lead's details by offering them something of value and enticing them to get in touch. Once you have their data, you can retarget them later via email marketing, providing they have consented to receive further marketing material from you.

Why a landing page works so well is that it's written to directly speak to a target audience, so you could have multiple landing pages, one for each campaign. For example, you could be offering cash flow advice to start-ups, but you may also want to offer other more specific services to more established businesses. Naturally, they would not respond to the same marketing content as one another. Each landing page should speak to the prospect, telling them you understand and empathise with their problems. It should also make perfectly clear that you are here to advise them whatever their stage of development. This can just be a simple statement of why your service is so great, maybe an endorsement or two from other clients. It can even be in the form of a headline. Keep it short and snappy. Don't think of it like an actual explanation of your services, think of it more of a goal your landing page must accomplish. This could just be the two or three key benefits which your firm has to offer.

Adding visual aids to make your landing page look as appealing as possible to your prospect is essential. In fact, I've witnessed some of the best conversion rates by adding large attention-grabbing images with less copy and more high-quality focused and relevant visuals. It's crucial to be clear and concise here. The last thing you want to do is confuse the visitor with too much copy. The focus is on making them interested in learning more in due course, via other more personal means of communication.

Build a Subscription List

You should look to **include a sign up form**. You want to build up that authority mentioned earlier and the best way to kick-start that is to begin creating a mailing list. You can then send out daily, weekly, or monthly emails to help keep your readers informed on say, accountancy best practice, recent relevant news and various other tips revolving around your business and your industry. This is easy to set up, using tools like Mailchimp to help create said mailing list and subscription forms.

Subscription lists or mailing lists are extremely powerful, and the reason why they work so well is that it allows you to build your credibility without being a pest. When you gain permission from the user to send them more information, you know they want to hear more about what you can offer them. This enables you to then cultivate more specific content for that audience, offering further value. Since most people who sign up are likely to be interested in improving their business and tax affairs, having a subscription list which allows you to market yourself as an expert is really effective.

Building a subscription list is simple. All you need to do is sign up to a tool such as aWeber or Mailchimp and then use the code provided on your website. More details of email marketing and using these tools are covered in Chapter 11. You can put the sign up form wherever you wish, though I'd recommend placing it toward the top or bottom of your website to capture interested parties. The best placement for the sign up box or form would very much depend on the style and layout of your site.

Done right, capturing the details of leads can go a long way to helping your firm secure more valuable contacts, and contracts. With a more refined and specific kind of mailing list you are better placed to upsell your most valuable services. There are more advanced bespoke software tools you can use to help improve conversion rates too. Our partner company uses AI powered platforms to understand individual client preferences. Instead of using generic email marketing templates, the software is able to generate more personalised and compelling marketing campaigns which achieve higher conversion rates than a standard piece of kit.

Install a Live Chat Service

You can use various website plugins and software tools to install a live chat system. What is a live chat system? They are interactive pop ups which appear on your site after someone arrives. I'm sure you've probably seen them before, they usually appear in the bottom right corner of the screen. Live chat systems allow you to catch a confused visitor who might have a pertinent question that they cannot find on your site. It's great for making introductions, building consensus and earning trust.

One of the main reasons why you should look to install a live chat system is that it enables you to capture leads without them leaving and going over to your competition. Chat options were once seen as just for retail firms, but accountants and professional service providers are highly likely to benefit from adding one. Indeed, companies such as LivePerson believe that a live chat service could improve your conversion rates by as much as one fifth alone. In fact, a few of my clients have seen conversion rates improve by as much as 30%, simply by implementing a chatbot.

The reason why this works so well is that, frankly, most people don't want to sit and talk on the phone. Having the time to think and thrash out what you want to say is very important in the modern world. Live chat programs encourage the user to reach out, but to reach out through a medium they are happy to work with. Someone might not know how to phrase their question in person but could more readily do so via email or live chat. I personally use live chat most of the time and find it can be a true time saver.

By offering you some basic chat details, any website visitor can start a conversation with you or a member of your accountancy firm in real time. This is great for making sure you can answer their questions and ensures you capture that all important interest by demonstrating your value. More importantly, it gives you the opportunity to collate some new leads which could later be turned into clients. Many chat plugins are available, depending on the platform you run your website through, so finding a chat program which works well for you should not be a problem. I'd recommend the likes of LivePerson, Zendesk, Bold360 or PureChat.

Installing one, though, can be incredibly beneficial. It's a useful way to engage with traffic and can prevent you from losing out on potentially valuable leads.

NICK'S TIPS

Learn to love live chat. Use the bots as additional sales soldiers for your firm. Not only are they likely to improve your sales, they are insightful too. Think about the questions your audience are asking, as this can be a great way of getting ideas to create useful blog posts.

Include an Introductory Video

Now you should look to **add in an introductory video to your homepage.** A video introduction is a great tactic for several reasons, as it allows you to sum up who you are and directly speak to your ideal client. It will be the first thing visitors will see when they arrive at your site, and therefore a big chance to really create a good impression as you connect with visitors. I can guarantee you many of your competitors won't be doing this which makes it an excellent opportunity for you to get ahead and stay in the mind of any prospect.

Why this works is simple: it puts a face to the business. Sure, you might not be a natural actor, but you are a respected professional knowing much about your profession and related subjects. You will immediately offer up a personality for yourself and your firm, making it easy to show each person who visits your website **who you are, what you are all about and why your firm is the best choice.** Most people cannot be bothered reading through content but will find a quick introductory video tells them all they need to know. So, you must take advantage of this and start showcasing your expertise, personality and trustworthiness as quickly as possible to capture potential leads.

It all comes down to two things: traffic and trust. Trust is critical and being able to put a face and voice to your business does a lot to help forge the trust you need from the get-go.

In terms of traffic, video is one of the most powerful ways of driving more traffic to a website. Considering over 80% of viewers prefer to watch a video than read text, coupled with the fact that Google owns YouTube, why would you not make use of video? It's one of the fastest ways to boost your site rankings from an SEO perspective and is a crucial traffic generator.

You have approximately ten seconds to keep someone onsite, so realistically your video must begin pretty impressively. Keep your recording to a couple minutes long, and you will find that it helps improve your conversion rate, as well as your bounce rate metric (more on this later). All of this will result in more positive clicks through to your website, resulting in a higher search engine ranking placement thanks to the optimisation boost video content garners. Awesome, right?

So, with that in mind, let's give you some tips on what to consider when shooting an introductory video. Your video should look to:

- Provide a clear explanation of who you are and what you offer.
- Set a clear tone for the specialist service(s) which you provide.
- Display your core values as a business and create interest.
- Connect on a more personal level, showing the prospective client you understand their pain points *and* have a solution for them.
- Showcase what it would be like for the client if they hired you.

Lastly, your video does one more thing you truly need: it puts the viewer on the path to converting. Simply direct them, via the video, to your site's most pivotal pages and key areas. Recommend that they sign up to your mailing list for more expert, free advice. Basically, invite them to where you want them to go next. After having watched the video, the worst thing you could have is a viewer thinking 'What now?'

Tell them! Let them know what you want them to do. Encourage them to look around the site, to share the video with fellow professionals and, most importantly, to get in touch.

It's for these simple reasons that turning to video makes such a good choice. It looks great, helps you to stand out, and makes you appear far more professional. But only when done right!

NICK'S TIPS

You don't need to spend huge amounts of money on video recording equipment to create appropriate videos for your firm. Simply see who has the best smartphone for filming in your office and you could shoot the video for free. Then just upload it to your website and test that it works properly using different devices.

Create a Mobile Friendly Responsive Website

Make sure you have a **responsive website that is mobile friendly.** A website which scales to the right size of screen is important, as a desktop specific website won't look good on a mobile screen and vice versa. With that in mind, you should look to ensure your website is built using a content management system such as WordPress, Magento or Joomla.

The reason why you need a working and highly responsive website across different devices is simple: Google ranks websites by looking at their mobile compatibility (known as 'Mobile First') as well as their security. The mobile aspect is very important indeed. Why? Because, put simply, Google cares more and more about results. With over half of your potential audience accessing the internet on their phones, it would be foolish to ignore the rationale behind this and not take into account.

This means that if your website is not responsive on either mobile or desktop platforms, you risk leaving potential business on the table as visitors will detract from your site and look elsewhere. Therefore, testing and monitoring the statistics behind each platform is essential. I'll cover measuring metrics in greater detail towards the end of the book.

Keep this in mind, as your display features will need to be both mobile friendly *and* run on an HTTPS platform: this is easy to do through your hosting provider. Most website developers can make it easy for your website to come to life, ensuring you can create a responsive site which mirrors your qualities on both desktop and mobile.

While you may struggle to design and develop a website on your own, if you outsource some of the work, make sure the importance of responsive design and page speed is covered. It will help to improve website ranking, ensuring it's accessible to all, and help to show that your business is tailored to both desktop and mobile users. You should also look to use the Google Page Speed Test for both mobile and desktop, which lets you know if your website performs as well on each one.

EXERCISE

Sit down with a few of your staff members in a meeting room and bring up your website on the big screen. See how well it measures up to what you've learned in this chapter and then compare it to some of your competitors' websites. Identify ways of how you could stand out from your competition by employing some of the above tactics

Now that you can see why website optimisation is critical to marketing your business effectively, let's look at how to populate your website with top quality content that encourages users to come back for more.

Takeaways

- You need to be ready to create a more methodical approach to your website. It's one of your most powerful marketing tools and should be designed, managed and used as such.
- You should look to build a cohesive well-structured story for your firm's website and implement some or all of the six major tactics to ensure your website is optimised smartly and impactfully.
- Everything from utilising a mailing list to implementing a landing page will help to establish trust and encourage leads and potential clients to come back to you in the future.
- Visitor interaction tools will always play a leading role in enabling you to outdo your competition if used correctly.
- A responsive website design will display your business in the right light to each potential client, regardless of the device they are using.
- You don't need to spend thousands on your website when it comes to the design: you should instead look to make your budget work towards optimising your present website to deliver better results.

CHAPTER 5

BLOGGING FOR BUSINESS

Previously, you discovered the value of structuring your online website to be an effective tool. Building and creating a strong, well-defined story of your business alongside optimising your website correctly is imperative. These elements and features will become an essential part of your marketing strategy and business growth.

Now that you feel more comfortable with the knowledge of how to establish a solid online foundation, it's time to move on to another very useful tool you should make the most of: **your business blog**. Blogging is easily among the most versatile and effective tools you have at your disposal. If your business is not running a blog at present, you really need to ask yourself why. This chapter will show you exactly why utilising a blog for your business is more than just a good idea, it's a necessity.

Your blog is the entry point to regular engagement with visitors that allows a 'cold' prospect to turn into a 'warm' one. You can demonstrate an understanding of their business and its issues, offering suggestions and advice, or answering queries which relate to your area of expertise. Visitors knew nothing about you on arrival but may leave believing you are the expert they needed. Perfect, right?

In this chapter, I'm going to show you the wider benefits of running a blog and look at a five-step process which will lead to the creation of a successful, professional blog, one that will prove to be valuable resource for its readers.

The rewards from running a good blog are measured by your ability to connect with your ideal client. When done correctly, a blog will become one of your most pertinent marketing tools. Used incorrectly though, you may find it produces very little in the way of results. Let's look at how you can avoid the latter and make the former much more likely.

What is a Blog?

Your blog is your own little hub and piece of the internet, a place to answer questions, provide insights and deliver professional commentary. It's your spotlight to show the world your expertise, to help your ideal client understand what makes you special, and to ensure your knowledge can be of benefit to the reader. It's your perfect means to locate, attract, entice, educate and inform your ideal client.

From a business perspective then, a blog is crucial to the success of your firm. If you are serious about building a business you can actively grow and improve, you need to help interested readers get more out of your blog.

Business blogging is very different to running a hobby one. It's supposed to be a representation of your professional voice and portray leading authority and expertise. This means that the tone, the topic choice and even how the content is optimised for visibility, are drastically different. At the same time, it's not a blog you will use purely to make money from directly. After all, this is not about affiliate or influencer marketing.

While your long-term aim may well be to create conversions, the primary objective for a business blog is to bring in traffic that will be interested in what you have to say. By giving your readers great content, you'll discover that people find it easier to trust what you say. Along the way, you'll need to engage your audience with regular content to entice them to return and see that you offer more solutions to various problems they may have. As they get more value from the resource you offer, they'll move further down the funnel, with the process turning them from a prospect into a lead, and eventually converting into a client.

With that in mind, it's also important to make sure you are consistent with how often you post. Posting three blog articles in a single week and then nothing for a month will do no good. It's better to post one or two articles per week, every week, as it helps people to see you are committed to offering value. If your blog is inconsistent and not regularly maintained, it hardly sets a good precedent for how you work as a professional. Keep that in mind: the **consistency of posting** is just as important as **the quality of posting**.

If you are serious about building a long-term future in the professional services industry, a blog is a reference guide you offer as part of the package. It attracts traffic, bringing visitors who are interested in finding out something in your field of interest. It's going to help you to interact with those who you can serve best, ensuring your business appears as tailor-made to solve the numerous problems they may encounter. For that reason, running a blog should be high on your list of priorities, even if you are not a natural writer (more on this shortly).

Business blogging is a very compelling and low-cost solution to getting your business spotted. But why do you really need one? What can it do for you?

Why do You Need a Blog?

The main purpose of your blog is **to help create awareness and boost engagement with your ideal client.** It should inform the reader and encourage them to take action through relevant information, detailed guidance and helpful advice. Rich content will, over time, lead to higher lead generation and better conversion rates overall.

The primary reason why you need a business blog is to drive traffic to your site and eventually create conversions. Informative blog content is going to influence people, giving them access to information which they may not find elsewhere. This is going to provide extra value to your readers, which should help them to move further down your marketing funnel, as shown in Fig. 5.1. Instead of just directly marketing a service to potential clients, you show them **why they need** the skills you offer. The aim is to consistently provide great value and engage with your readers at every stage of their buying journey. Drawing in visitors, building your readership and encouraging prospects to convert to clients takes time and is not an overnight occurrence. The key is to be consistent in providing rich content which is fresh, topical, relevant and of high-quality.

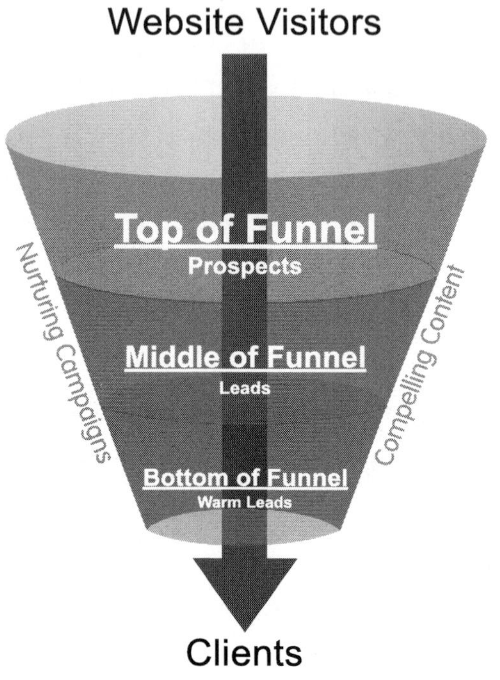

Figure 5.1

Your website should have a series of blog posts which are optimised to fit in with your marketing goals and speak directly to your ideal client. This also allows you to gain better search engine rankings when individuals are looking for specific keywords that resonate with your blog (more on this in Chapter 7 where I'll cover optimisation). A blog is beneficial as it enables you to run your promotional articles, topical content, informational pieces and advice columns all in one place. It saves the rest of your website from looking cluttered and makes it easy for readers to find and locate those of your blog pieces that best apply to their present predicament.

Blogging for business is the single strongest solution you have to develop trust, authority and confidence. Through your blog, it becomes much easier to give your readers information and advice they can learn from and use to their advantage. This is easily among your most viable marketing tools, helping you to break the mould and stand out from the competition. Do you remember I mentioned earlier about the importance of standing out from the crowd and about having your own Unique Selling Point (USP)? Well, one of the most potent selling points you can have is an informative and detailed blog, designed to arm every reader with the information they need to move forward, as well as encouraging them to use your services.

The Benefits of Business Blogging

Like any other marketing tool for your business, the benefits of blogging mainly come in the shape of attracting new leads and eventually procuring more clients. Ideally, attracting those clients who are perfectly suited to your short-term and long-term goals. However, some of the other common benefits of having a business blog include:

- **Increased traffic and visibility.** Blogging will gain you a more consistent stream of traffic from those visitors primed by an interest in your business services. Instead of getting traffic which might not relate, a blog helps to boost those visitors whose search queries relate to the contents of your blog, increasing your visibility to the kind of people you want to connect with.
- **Showcase your qualities.** As an accountant or other type of professional, standing out from the crowd can be tough to achieve. You should use your blog to work almost as a portfolio of your expertise. Proof of success is essential, so use this space to include everything from previous success stories to creating data-driven content which shows your commitment, dedication and passion.
- **Help your business grow.** Of course, while I mentioned the Pareto Principle earlier, where 80% of your best work comes from 20% of your clients, you still want the total number to grow. Blogging is a great way to start connecting with your audience and drawing

more engagement with ideal clients, simply by offering them content which promotes the very solution they are in search of.

- **Give your business an edge over the competition.** Part of the benefit of running a business blog is that you can offer more insight to readers than your competitors, highlighting your particular areas of expertise. While the content will probably have to solve many common problems, you can also use it to help people see the benefits of additional services and skills offered to them. Blogs are great for creating desire.
- **Create content which produces results long-term.** Many forms of marketing which you take part in often provide a short-term boon before needing to be refreshed. With a blog, that one post could still be bringing you traffic in a decade's time. The majority of views on a blog will be looking at older content, so don't feel like every article has to deliver within a few weeks of it being uploaded. Good content will deliver returns in the long-term.

Now, let's look at how to use your blog to consistently deliver your marketing message and reach. Your blog must deliver interesting and relevant information to the reader, as well as entice more traffic to your website. **Every good blog helps to encourage the reader to take action and hire your professional skills and services.**

How to Create a Blog Which Helps Your Firm Grow

Until now, I've concentrated heavily on the importance of hooking your 'ideal client'. Now it's time to put that profile you built to good use. When creating your blog, you should build your content around **what this ideal client would want you to write about.** So, let's say you're an accounting firm specialising in helping tech start-ups with cash flow. Your blog posts should be built around common questions and concerns on that topic.

Another key part of creating a worthwhile blog is that it must be planned out accordingly. If you intend to upload a new post every Tuesday, then you ought to begin research around the topic days in advance. Simply having a quick skim around on a Monday night or a Tuesday morning will not be enough. Great blogs are successful because they are in-depth, well-researched and planned effectively.

It's critical you spend some time getting used to the art of planning your blog. As the old saying goes, if you fail to plan then you should plan to fail. Your content is supposed to inspire, so it must be worth reading, otherwise it will be hard to make use of the many benefits that a blog offers.

Creating the blog plan and outline takes a huge amount of work, time and effort. Luckily for you though, I've put together some good ideas below in the form of a **five-step process.** This will guide you through building the foundations of a business blog which will assist you in **retaining clients, attracting new clients** and **converting more clicks into clients**. Sound good?

Where Should You Start?

Maximise the impact of your content by making sure the topic is as evergreen as possible. While you should always look to include short-term articles which are seasonal or topical, having a long list of evergreen topics makes a lot of sense. These could be anything from the five most common questions you get asked by IT contractors, to the FAQs you come across when running 'contractor accountants' Google Trends searches.

Before going any further think about the following questions:

- Does your ideal client have a particular goal that you wish to help them achieve? Or a problem you wish to help them solve? Maybe something unique to their industry or market?
- Is your business blog structured to be a resource for those interested in your field? Does it present a mix of information that gives guidance on various common issues?

- In relation to the previous point are the articles relevant to the readers' demographics? Keep that in mind, as you could be creating awesome content which isn't suitable for your target audience.
- What might cause the ideal client for your business not to use your service? What kind of barriers should you be breaking down with instructive, value-driven articles? Consider your USP here.

Over time make use of analysis tools to help you see which posts draw in new readers and which are the most referred to. Using Google Analytics, for example, you can get advanced information about how each visitor is engaging with your website. This lets you see the content delivering traffic from search queries, but it also helps you to identify weaknesses and points where improvements must be made.

Analytic tools let you delve further into how individuals are interacting with you on your website. More on this later. For now, it's enough to appreciate that you:

a) need an ideal target audience and,

b) must work out the best way to entice those individuals to engage with your articles/content.

For a good quality blog to come to life, you often need to do a fair amount of work to make that possible. If you want to start putting in place the steps toward maintaining a high standard blog, there are five fundamentals you must consider. Each of these will play a role in making sure your blog feels professional and, more critically, ensures the content produces lasting, positive results for your business.

How then, can you go about creating a high-quality blog that makes the right impression? Let's begin looking at the five-step process which will play a deciding role in the success of your blog. The process of forward planning allows you to understand **who you are targeting, why you are targeting them** and **what reasons they might have** for reading your blog in the first place.

With this in mind, it becomes much easier to create something special. Let's start with step one: finding the best writer for your blog. Sometimes, that might not be you.

Step One: Deciding on Who Should Write the Content for Your Blog

The first big challenge you face is determining who will write the content for your blog. Some firms will look to do their own in-house writing to ensure the accuracy and completeness of any article. If this is your concern then you should look to create an editorial system that works for you.

Many professionals will request a content writer to source interesting industry topics built around their target audience. Then they will have the writer create the copy, and the in-house reviewer would simply read over it and professionalise the language, topic and content. Finding good quality content writers is relatively easy, you have a few options:

- You can advertise for content writers on your website, asking for those who write in your field to apply.
- Freelancing websites and LinkedIn can be used to source writers that may be available to hire.
- You could turn to specialist writers with portfolios and ask them directly if they would be interested in writing on your topic.
- Alternatively, use an agency which provides content writing services specifically for the industry which you work in.

Typically, you'll find you either need to pay for exposure or you need to pay for content. Just remember that you often get what you pay for: if you go for the cheapest writer, don't expect a heavily referenced, fact-driven, authoritative and professional piece. If you choose to use a specialist writer, you will often have to pay premium rates, especially if the content required is on a particular subject or niche topic. If you use an agency, you would typically expect to be charged anything from 10p per word. Generally, the more in-depth and specific your requirements are, the more you can anticipate it will cost.

Most of the time, even when hiring a trusted and professional writer, you'll need to review the article or blog post as a first draft to begin with.

It can be a frustrating process and a bit of a struggle at the outset. I'd recommend that you establish some clear guidelines in the form of a writing brief when sourcing each writer. This should allow you to more readily tap into the standards you expect and cover factors such as:

- The kind of content you wish to receive, with a list of acceptable topics and subtopics.
- A headline, a working title and an outline to show the writer what you want the article to include and/or exclude.
- The types of imagery which can and cannot be used within the content, including image size limits.
- Detailed formatting, writing and layout guidelines to help reduce editing time and disputes.
- Examples of acceptable content and, where possible, examples of unacceptable content.
- Suggest the keywords you want to be included as these are what drives traffic to your website from Google searches.

The more detailed the above, the more likely it is that you will see lasting success moving forward. You should look to supply any writers with clear instructions about what you require, your target audience and the kind of content you expect to receive from them. This saves you wasting time and money.

When working with a writer make sure there is an understanding of expectations prior to the writing beginning. Agree upon a price and a turnaround time, working out a timescale plan for edits and adjustments. Ensure you communicate on things like guidelines, editing styles, deadlines and budgets at the beginning so you can avoid much of the stress involved in hiring a writer.

Step Two: Creating Informative, Worthwhile Content

Now, the one thing you have to understand here is that your content must follow a predictable path. Marketers might tell you that predictability is going to hurt you, but not for a professional firm. You want to develop a readership who come back to visit and read your blog regularly. Your audience want to become familiar with you and your content. This means changes in the format, tone and style every few months is going to look amateurish.

Instead, it's better to try and create what is known as a segmented content structure. It's like a themed kind of post. For example, an accountancy firm could run regular 'Taxation Tuesday' posts, where every Tuesday the blog could look at a specific taxation problem and explain the HMRC terminology and current rates of tax applicable on this. In that same post, you are offering value *and* letting the reader know they could benefit from further advice if they hire you. By running this kind of thematic style, you create a predictable level of appeal where readers will check in as they know when you release an article which may be of interest to them.

Your content should follow this kind of release style. All your content too, not just your blog. From Webinar Wednesdays to Form Filling Fridays, you can create all manner of themed blog post variations which can be uploaded at regular intervals, weekly or monthly, to generate familiarity. This allows you to create a lot of content around specific topics that you know people want to learn more about.

If you choose to write all your content yourself, it's critical you get to grips with the impact of any article's headline. **A good headline catches the**

attention of the reader, brings up a problem, and then offers the solution. A bad headline offers vague information with only a hint of greater detail within, which potential readers may not consider to be relevant or of much interest to them.

The most important thing you can do as an accountant is to tap into the mindset of your ideal client. For example, if you wanted to target IT companies with cash flow issues, a simple but effective headline for this could be *'How can I stop cash flow woes for my IT business?'*

It's basic, yes, but it's entirely self-explanatory. Anyone reading that is going to understand 100% what you want them to learn about. *'5 Ways You Can Cut Down on Cash Flow Problems for Your IT Business'* is another take on the same idea.

Your headlines should always be built around trying to gain interest and entice clicks. Other good headline styles are ones which interest the reader, promising to inform them on the chosen topic. *'3 Easy Ways to Understand Cash Flow for your IT Business'* would be a suitable article title to spill some trade secrets about better grasping cash flow, while promising further professional consultation. Tough? Yes, very. Possible? Almost certainly.

However, it's important to state that **if you feel like you are not a natural writer, don't stress yourself out**. Others can help you with the writing side of things, if you so wish. As an accountant, you'll naturally have a knack for numbers, so writing articles and blogs might not be for you. Besides, the last thing you want to be accused of is 'creative accounting' right? Bad joke. Sorry. Moving on swiftly then, if you're not a natural born writer, you shouldn't write off your use of a blog. It's definitely one of your most valuable marketing and brand building tools. It just means you need to look for outside assistance.

NICK'S TIPS

Good ways of finding ideas to create informative, worthwhile content could include; checking out forums, live chats, reviews, relevant industry blogs and using tools such as Google Trends to help you discover the most popular topics in your industry.

Google Trends is a handy tool. With a simple search term, you can see the long-term popularity and search volume for a particular topic, which is great for finding useful short-term and long-term content.

Step Three: Keeping the Standard Consistent

Of course, any professional blog worth reading in your industry must be in good condition with content standards kept consistent. It should be made up of a host of unique content, covering all manner of short, medium and long-term questions, subjects and topics.

You should aim to deliver a blog which has the specific tone and theme you wish to put across. If you specialise in one area of taxation, then you would naturally want to push consistent content on the problems and solutions revolving around that subject area. Maintain a list which includes all the key points of your posts, current and future. If you keep the following in mind for all pieces you write, then they will fit with the aims and ideology of your business:

- Work out what your primary goal is. It might be to help local businesses expand without consuming their cash flow. If so, you should start by making sure all your blog content is built around this specialist topic.

- Think about the kind of information your ideal client would like to read about. Are they likely to favour statistical information? Case studies? Show and tell? Anecdotes? Find out what inspires your reader more and concentrate on that form of writing.

- Think about the typical age of people that you target. For example, if your accountancy firm specialises in helping start-ups grow, then you could look to have a more youthful tone. Where a firm is targeting experienced industry pros then it's better to adopt a more formal one. Keeping the consistency of tone is as necessary as the consistency of the message.
- Also consider what might be holding your ideal client back from making a definitive decision. What could *you do* to help make them feel comfortable in saying 'yes' to your business? What kind of content and messaging tends to make this point to them?

This is arguably the most abstract part of running a blog, as well as being pertinent to drawing in the right audience. If you can maintain a voice and a soul which stays consistent in terms of messaging and theme, you will be much more likely to keep your readers engaged.

You don't want to be repetitive, but you also don't want to try and cover all the bases in accountancy. Your blog should speak naturally, in a certain way, to a certain kind of client. **Every good blog has a voice and a style of its own. You need to find yours, based on what your ideal client desires**. If they want a more upbeat, informal style of accountancy, it pays to deliver that. If they want formal professionalism, you should tailor your blog to fit accordingly. Whatever voice you choose, keep it consistent throughout your posts and content.

Step Four: SEO Optimised Content

One thing you may need to get familiar with is the concept of creating search engine optimised (SEO) content. I'll cover SEO in more detail as the book goes on, but for now it's important to appreciate that **SEO content is essential**, as this is what makes your blog posts rank higher than the competition's. Each blog post should contain at least the following:

- A headline, which uses your primary keyword (more on this later). Good headlines are critical to draw in the reader.
- A 'meta' description, which is a short, 2-3 sentence long description of what the article is primarily about.
- Body text, which will be the main text of the article. Split this up into sections of 250-300 words, using subheadings to keep the content easy to read.
- An image which uses the primary keyword as its 'alt' attribute. Search engines can't read images, so you have to include an 'alt' for it to determine what the image is.

You should also include links to other relevant content from your blog. At the same time, look to reference recognised sources, such as publications or official government documentation, and other experts to help reinforce the veracity of key points being made. Make sure your references come from well-respected sources, keeping the tone authoritative.

Step Five: Auditing Your Blog Posts

Lastly, you can monitor the progress of your blog posts. The easiest way to do this is by using tools like Google Analytics. These allow you to easily follow the results of each blog post, seeing how often individuals are using your website and how receptive each article is to your audience. Another great tool you can use is Buzzsumo, which is incredibly useful for measuring the rough metrics of your content engagement. You can quickly see what content is resonating with your target audience by paying attention to data on the average number of shares for particular content topics or posts.

Of course, if results are not quite as fruitful as you would have expected, that can flag up a problem. Finding out where the problem lies can be difficult. So here are some things you could investigate on each blog post to try and determine if it's the culprit for any lower than expected results:

- First look at the title of the article. Does it hold a primary keyword? Does it ask a question and then propose an answer?
- Read through all the text within the article. Does the text inform the reader? Does it make use of the correct keywords naturally?
- What about your images? Are they placed in the right locations? Are they tagged with the correct image 'alt' attributes?
- Does the URL match up with the actual topic of a post? Does it include a keyword wherever possible?

You will appreciate that as you increase your blog posts they will need to be categorised over time. This stops your FAQ posts being lost in amongst your themed posts and allows for better compartmentalisation of the whole blog. By categorising your blog, your audience can more readily find those articles which match their own interests or answer a burning question which may have prompted their visit to your site. It's important to ensure the blog is easy to navigate for readers, creating a more pleasant user experience.

Be sure to get familiar with using tools such as Google Analytics, to see performance statistics for each blog post. If you wish to increase them, try carrying out an audit on the above features: it might just prove to be the solution you need.

EXERCISE

Get together with your staff members and discuss your own blog. Is it currently ticking all the boxes? Think of ways you can implement the five steps above to your blog posts and see how well they are doing using the tools mentioned. Compare your blog to those of your competitors. Where would you rank yourself compared to them?

Now, creating rich and detailed content for your blog is going to be tough, even if you outsource the process. You should, therefore, look to make the right choice from the beginning. **Done right, a blog will always be a unique source of traffic, reputational management and authority building.**

What else can you do to help build up your visibility and authority? You can use more direct forms of marketing, such as Pay-Per-Click (PPC) marketing. **Let's look at PPC marketing now.**

Takeaways

- Creating a blog is paramount to your long-term visibility and influence. It will help you stand out from the crowd by showcasing your expertise.
- Your business blog should have conversion as the end goal and look to move your visitors through the marketing funnel, taking them from prospects to leads to clients.
- Each blog piece must speak to your ideal client in some way. They should always be informative, interesting and relevant.
- You do not have to write all your content yourself, but if you are outsourcing content creation be sure to give clear guidelines.
- Your content should be rich, varied, thematic and predictable in its layout and structure.
- Your blog posts should be consistent in tone and regularity, adding to your story and enhancing your marketing message.

CHAPTER 6

PAID SEARCH AND GOOGLE ADS

The last chapter covered the key aspects of running a blog on your website and how empowering a business blog can be for your firm. As a professional services provider, it's imperative that you can showcase your expertise and knowledge to your ideal client. Now you know how to go about posting killer content to make a positive impression and you have a greater understanding of what you should include on your website, let's move into the paid search marketing side of things.

In this chapter, I'll touch heavily on **Paid Search**, otherwise known as **Pay-Per-Click (PPC).** I will outline what this involves, how to set it up and why it could be your most useful companion. PPC marketing is a hugely powerful tool, although if used incorrectly, it could become very expensive with little return. You'll learn what PPC is designed for, when to consider investing in it, and how you can best use it to your advantage as a professional.

What is Paid Search (PPC)?

Paid marketing is a broad term which covers anything from search engine marketing (SEM), to search engine optimisation (SEO), search engine advertising and sponsored content. However, one of the more effective forms of paid marketing is known as *paid search marketing* or *pay-per-click (PPC)*.

Paid search marketing is all about helping you to use the sponsored listings on a search engine or a website. When you type in a word or query into a search engine like Google, your screen will display a list of relevant search results. Some of those options at the top of the list are paid for, meaning that they are sponsored by a business for advertising purposes.

Sponsorship is used to help a business gain exposure and to bring in traffic. For every click onto a sponsored link, the search engine charges a pre-agreed price for this. As you can imagine, that can have a double-edged sword feel to it. It can be profitable if it works to your advantage. On the other hand, too many clicks without a great website behind it may cause visitors to leave without taking any further action, costing you money without any business gain.

However, with an optimised website and an engaging blog, that isn't necessarily the case. It's important to keep this in mind, as you need to have something worthwhile to make your pay-per-click advertising give a return on the money which you are paying out in the first place.

At the top of any search results you receive from a search query you will notice some listings that are marked with an 'Ad' icon, this is where your own sponsored listing would appear, for the search terms you choose to rank for. For example, you could create a paid search ad for 'accountant in LOCATION', with the location naturally being the area you wish to target.

Anyone searching for that would then see your sponsored link and if they clicked through to it, you would then pay a set fee for the click, hence pay-per-click. Of course, the quality of your ad and various other factors will come into play when determining your positioning in the search engine listings.

However, there is another element in play here: paid search marketing is just a marketing term. How do you actually register with a search engine to get your advertisements to appear? Simple: **Google Ads.**

What are Google Ads?

Some might know it as Google AdWords, it's really the same thing. This is the self-made advertising platform that Google operates, a system which supports the 'Ad' results section I've just mentioned. For a set fee per click, your listing will appear high on the search results in Google for a specific term, the keyword of a query. This will most likely be something to do with your core business. Take a look at Fig. 6.1 below, which is a good example of Google Ads in action.

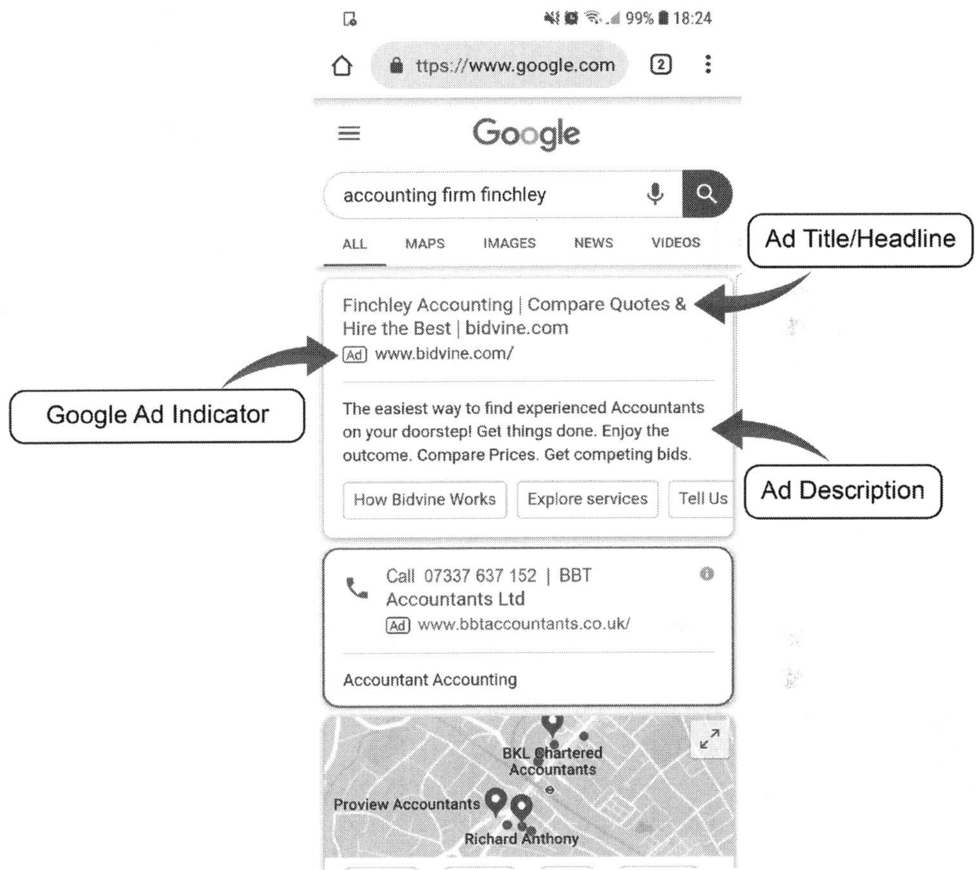

Figure 6.1

As you can see from Fig. 6.1, by typing the words 'accounting firm Finchley' into Google on my mobile device, I am immediately presented with a couple of Google Ads that appear at the very top of the listings, along with a Google My Business search map. The sponsored links are denoted with small 'Ad' letters highlighted in green with a rectangular border. Depending on whether you are browsing on a mobile, tablet or laptop, the ads could also appear on the right-hand side or toward the bottom of the search results. They can be in multiple places but the important thing to remember is, they will have the word 'Ad' next to them in some way, shape or form. Sometimes the ad icon may appear less conspicuously and on other occasions stand out in bright orange. It really depends on how Google is feeling from time to time.

The ad that appears here is for BBT Accountants. The ad above BBT Accountants is not a firm – it's just an ad for a company sourcing platform. It's important to think about how your ad description might be better worded to gain a good ranking position in Google. Here in BBT's case, having a number as a Call-to-Action is great, but it's better to use this in conjunction with an optimised, descriptive headline or ad title for maximum conversion.

Speaking of which, there are no keywords whatsoever used in the headline displayed here. It just has the name of the firm and contact number in it. As a prospect, I would also like to know what they can offer me from looking at an ad. If there are no keywords or anything compelling or enticing, the chances are I am going to ignore that ad and continue browsing. Not including a catchy headline or some description of your services shows a lack of care and disinterest in potential clients. I would most likely scroll down to see which other ads are more enticing, trying to find ones that I can be sure offer the professional services I want or answer the question which prompted my search in the first place. Then I would most likely be ready to switch screens to make the all-important call.

Am I more likely to click on an ad which is descriptive and speaks directly to me or click on an ad with no description, one that does not show what I am looking for? You simply cannot afford to miss a step when optimising your Google Ads if you want quality leads!

I'll focus on optimisation and keywords shortly, but it's important to keep them in mind for now.

While you could also run your ads through other search engines, it's safe to say that Google Ads is probably the best PPC campaign manager around. Google is the largest search engine by far, so it's likely you will get the most hits for your business by designing your advertising to best fit their criteria.

Google Ads works by enabling you to select specific keywords you wish to draw your primary target's attention to. Based on all manner of factors, such as the popularity of the term and the competition of those advertising for that term, you will pay a set fee per click. Then you need to write an enticing ad which makes someone want to click through to your new and improved website. You should create an ad to capture ideal clients, with landing pages tailored to fit those clients with the information and guidance they want to see.

It's important to remember that simply buying a Google Ads slot will not guarantee you hits. If your website is of a poor standard, Google will prioritise others ahead of you in the listings. This means that ensuring the quality of your website and optimising it with at least the six tactics I mentioned earlier, is essential. Google will create what is known as an 'Ad Rank' for your advertisement, so you should ensure you have crafted it to tick as many boxes as possible.

An 'Ad Rank' is a value that's used to determine your ad position. It considers things like the quality of the ad itself, the use of ad extensions and the context of the search in relation to the query. These factors all help Google determine where ads should be shown on a page relevant to other ads. For example, trying to get yourself spotted as an accountant by ranking in ads for health professionals is not likely to gain you many points with Google. If your ad is relevant to your industry, which it should be, it's likely to gain a good position in the search engine results page (SERP).

You then need to get used to the bidding process, where you indicate how much you are willing to pay for each click. When you register with Google Ads for sponsorship you are competing with others who have also signed up. You can set a maximum bid amount so where other competitors' bids exceed that amount you automatically drop out, avoiding spending too much and blowing your budget. This all happens and is accounted for in a fraction of a second, so you often see fast results. You want to see a return on the cost of any extra traffic you gain from improved visibility.

But why should you choose to advertise your firm using Google Ads?

Why Should You Use Google Ads?

As a professional who dreamed of starting your own firm, did you ever think of how you would get spotted by potential clients? Most accountants prior to the internet era were using classified ads to get noticed, relying on local media to build exposure. Well, think of Google Ads as the always online, always changing rebrand of classified ads. As you are only paying out when someone responds to your ad, it does mean that you can see more active results.

Using Google Ads enables you to bring in some instant traffic to your business. Unlike other advertising platforms where you could be waiting weeks, if not months, to see results, Google Ads posts your new advert almost immediately. With a high enough bid and an ample budget, you can be seen on Page 1 of Google for more or less any keyword of your choice in an incredibly short timeframe.

Therefore, you can see the response and measure the impact of your ads campaign on traffic soon after you start running it. Your ad might get seen by 1000 people, but only a fraction of them may end up contacting your firm. If you know this information from the outset you can start optimising and testing your ad campaigns accordingly to achieve the best results.

Also, the instant traffic you can achieve this way helps to improve your natural page ranking too. With ads, you have a better chance of seeing your website put on Page 1 of Google within a few clicks. It's one of the fastest ways of getting yourself some prime estate on Page 1 and appear to millions of people with not a great deal of effort.

It's great for generating new leads, especially at certain times of the year when demand is high for your services, such as tax year end.

Since your ideal client is likely out there trying to find the help they need, they'll be more likely to opt for a Page 1 result: most people trust Google's search results, after all. When individuals are actively searching for the keyword terms you are now ranking so highly for, thanks to Google Ads, it's much more likely your ideal client will then see you, click on your link and get in touch.

So, not only are you going to appear faster and rank higher – you'll be more likely to bring in the *exact* type of people you want to target. I'm sure you can appreciate just how powerful it can be. Unlike other forms of marketing where you hope the viewer is looking for you, Google Ads makes sure you are only appearing in response to relevant searches, tailored to fit.

Another key reason why you should use Google Ads is, put simply, you get what you pay for. If your ad is good and it gets a lot of clicks, you'll need to pay for those clicks. If nobody clicks (which is incredibly unlikely), you'll pay nothing. Sure, you then need those clicks to turn into leads and conversions, but as I've mentioned, it's all about building a good campaign to encourage those who arrive onsite to stick around.

If someone is interested enough to click on your ad, there's a good chance you can give them the guidance that they need and encourage them to get in touch. With Google Ads generating your firm plenty of leads, it's then up to you to respond to any interest and convert them.

Lastly, using Google Ads lets you target key geographic areas. This means that you are able to set a radius for your ad to show in search results for certain locations. Thus, when people from your designated area start searching for the keyword(s) your ad campaign targets, and they are in this catchment area, they'll see it.

Alongside having total control over how much value you get back from an ads campaign, you can make sure only the right individuals get in touch.

This means you aren't wasting resources appearing in cities and towns outside your area: with an actual radius set on a map, your firm is seen more predominantly by local people and businesses.

Since you are likely to be targeting a narrow area from which to draw in clients, you may not have to worry about excessive competition for the bidding on this within Google Ads. There probably aren't too many firms in your vicinity also using it. You need to be careful with your bidding, but fear not, you're about to discover how you can make the most of your Google Ad campaigns.

Let's look at that now.

NICK'S TIPS

You could run some Google Ads at certain times of the year to capitalise on new business acquisition when demand for your services peaks. For example, running ad campaigns for a few months before January 31st to target those who have to meet the self-assessment tax deadline.

Creating Your First Advertisement Using Google Ads

Firstly, head on over to Google Ads. Simply search for it or visit ads.google.com and create an account. You'll need to provide details like your country of origin and currency of choice. Once you do that, you'll be inside the Google Ads dashboard. Google even gives you a simple little wizard to follow, making sure you pick up some of the basics. Simply hit the button which reads 'Create Your First Campaign' and you can begin the process of campaign creation.

Follow these steps to create you first advertisement with Google Ads:

1. To get started, you should begin by naming your campaign. This is just for your own reference, so don't worry too much about what to call the campaign. It's just for easy differentiation of your campaigns.

2. Next, you will need to set up the language you wish to promote the campaign in and choose the locations you want to target. Make this as selective as you can: as you probably know where your target market is situated.

3. Now, simply set your location and your target audience. Be sure to dig deeper into the country options, as you'll be able to choose things like regions and cities. Simply type in your address and then allow this to be shown, as it makes those seeing the ad recognise where you are based.

4. Then, select the radius you wish the advert to be shown within, moving out from your own location. Take the time necessary to really consider this. Choosing too large a catchment area might result in a lot of wasted clicks. Too small and you might hamper the quality of reach for your advertisement.

5. You should now look at setting the campaign budget, one of the most vital parts of establishing an effective campaign. You can set daily, weekly and monthly limits. This is an entirely personal choice based on your own professional capacity, which you have to consider carefully according to your business needs and the budget available to you.

6. At this stage you are ready to write your first basic ad. It's essential to match your ad as closely as you can to your keywords. This can draw the attention of individuals who search for those words, showing your ad as being related to what they want.

7. Next, you should consider using location extensions, which enables you to include a link to your Google My Business account. If you do not have a Google My Business account, you ought to get one now: it's a fine way to make sure your business is recognised as a professional firm.

8. Lastly, use the call extensions feature to show your contact phone number within your ads listing. When your call extensions are visible, users can click a button to call your business directly, or they can click on your ad to go to your website. Either way, it increases your chances of getting and tracking valuable leads.

If you follow these steps, you are far more likely to get the most out of your Google Ads experience. However, there are some other very important factors you must consider, such as selecting keywords. **Let's look at how to make the most of your keyword planning now: this is an essential step to implementing a strong and rewarding PPC campaign.**

Getting to Grips with Keyword Research

While keyword research is a book worthy topic in its own right, it's essential to look at how to get you 'keyword ready' for campaign control. As you can imagine, some of your most commonly used keywords will be around your location and profession. For example, things like 'accountants in LOCATION' & 'LOCATION accountants' would make good starting points.

Thanks to the awesome Google Keywords Planner, you can see just how useful and affordable each keyword will be. Simply head to the 'Tools' tab in the Google Ads manager, and then select the Keyword Planner tool. Here, you type in a keyword and you'll be shown other related keywords, along with their monthly search volumes. The volume refers to the amount of times a keyword has come up in search queries over the past month. Be sure to use the filter in the tool to adjust it for your own country; as you'll probably only be interested in local or national results.

Always check the 'Local Monthly Searches' tab when looking at keyword analysis as it's your most useful and pertinent tab. Start working through the keyword suggestions, noting down the ones with a significant search volume and which most accurately describe your business. Remember to look for other names for an accountant too, such as 'tax expert' and 'bookkeeper' among any other terms which might be used locally.

This may help you to refine the language that you select for your ad. You may never refer to yourself as a 'tax specialist' but if it gets a lot of local searches, it might be time to begin doing so!

The challenge is to find keywords which are relevant to your business and bring in sufficient search volume per month with relatively low competition. Continuously build up your list of accountancy keywords, keeping a list of everything you can think of, terms like 'accounting', 'accountancy', 'auditor', 'tax service', 'tax preparation', etc. Do this exercise regularly and you'll have a fine list of keywords which could potentially be used to help with your Google search rankings.

Armed with this list of keywords, you can run multiple specific PPC campaigns via Google, all targeting your ideal clients in different ways. Try and run multiple ad campaigns simultaneously varying them by adopting slightly different keywords for your services so they cover the full range of those you wish to promote to your ideal client. You may have some overlap with your best keywords appearing more than once but that is to be expected.

If you want to make sure you only appear for an exact term in a search query, not a combination of the terms, you can do that too. If you were set to rank for 'LOCATION accountant' then you may wish to instead rank for 'accountant LOCATION' – and the reason why is simple. With the quotation marks included, this becomes what is known as an **Exact Match** and will ensure you only appear for that term as it's spelt out. Without the quotation marks, you would appear in any searches which contain both of those words, although not necessarily in that order. This could mean getting a lot of wasted clicks from irrelevant traffic.

Another keyword tip for you is to make use of avoided or negative search terms. This allows you to exclude specific terms to cut down on poor matches. As you hunt through all the potential keywords to rank for, you will probably notice lots of terms you wish to avoid. If you don't want to be recognised for bookkeeping, for example, you could include 'bookkeeping' or 'bookkeeper' and similar related terms under the Negative Keywords section in your Campaigns tab.

By doing this Google Ads will no longer show you in listings for search terms which involve those key phrases, helping you to cut down on wasted clicks and wasted money.

EXERCISE

Write down a list of 10-20 keywords you think best describe your firm and the services you offer. Now using the Google Keyword Planner, try and figure out how you can refine your list by choosing high search volume keywords with relatively low competition. Use the newly identified keywords in your PPC campaigns and measure how they do against other terms.

How to Use Google Ads to Your Advantage

Now that you understand the challenge of getting spotted with Google Ads, you need to actually write some ads. As I mentioned in Chapter 5, it's not always a job you can do, or wish to do, yourself. If you are not confident about this and worry you will waste more money through trial and error, it pays to invest some of your marketing budget into a professional Google Ads expert. They will have a better appreciation of what search queries you want to appear in if you provide them your keyword list, although they should be able to carry out keyword research too. They can then create quality ads which resonate with these keywords accordingly. With only 30 characters for your headline, you need to be smart about the language and number of characters you use for this.

If you choose to write the ads yourself, then consider the following:

- A good headline will often be built around **answering a clear question**. For example, you could rank for something like, *'Filing* *your tax return this month? Need help?.'* It's simple and points out a problem and a solution in one quick phrase.

- Remember that **the ad itself must be good**, as well as the headline. In your first few words you have to grab the reader's attention by introducing a problem and then offering a solution, or at the very least the hint of a solution. Get used to doing that, as it encourages the reader to click.

- Every good ad campaign you run will be built upon the importance of talking to the client. Avoid saying stuff like *'We can help you!',* without being harsh, the prospect does not yet care about you. Structure it around **helping them** for the best effect. Your campaign should look to speak to the exact problem they face, not merely tell the visitor you are here to help. They want to know, first and foremost, what benefits they will receive from using your service.

- Try and make **an offer which encourages them to click** through. It could be anything from a free consultation to promising to help reduce expenditure by X%. Just make sure you can live up to whatever claims you make!

However, remember that none of this even matters if your landing pages and websites are not optimised to a campaign's tailored audience to begin with. For example, a campaign targeted towards sole traders and self-assessment should navigate that audience to a landing page related to this topic, which displays straightforward advice around what they need to do, followed by a Call-to-Action. For every Google Ad you run, a bespoke landing page targeting the same keywords and overall message should be created if you wish to make the right impression. Your homepage might not be enough to speak to a specific audience, so it's essential to have landing pages which can solve the issue that a particular campaign's target audience is concerned with.

Now that I have covered a large portion of what you need to know about keyword management and writing PPC ads without depleting your budget, it's time to move on to another persuasive form of online marketing. **Let's look at the secrets to using search engine optimisation (SEO) to your advantage**. Done right, it will only help you out with your PPC ads. So, don't start creating anything until you have read the next chapter!

Takeaways

- Paid for advertising is a high-risk marketing solution if you are unsure of what to do. But in the right hands it can be an immensely powerful marketing tool.
- The level of control you have about where, when and how your ad should be displayed in listings far outstrips that of its traditional predecessor: the classified ads pages of a newspaper.
- However, getting the accuracy and the writing style correct is essential to ensure you attract the visitors you are targeting. Excessively broad advertising will cost you more and deliver unwanted traffic.
- If you are at all uncertain of what you are doing, you should bring in a specialist to help you make the right choices around PPC marketing.
- With a bit of research into keyword usage you can ensure your Google Ads campaign is applied very selectively, only being seen by your desired target audience.

CHAPTER 7

SEARCH ENGINE OPTIMISATION: IS YOUR WEBSITE RANKING ON THE FIRST PAGE OF GOOGLE?

Earlier, I focused on the impact of using paid search advertising to increase traffic and improve your visibility. It's a good tool in your marketing kit and paid search solutions often work to your benefit.

That said, another important marketing tool you need to have working for you is **Search Engine Optimisation (SEO)**. In this chapter I'm going to get straight into the importance of using SEO so you can work towards building a more cohesive structure for your campaign. This is a subject which has many books dedicated to explaining how it works in great detail at a more advanced level. I am simply going to cover the principles of SEO best practice here, enabling you to implement basic SEO almost immediately.

I touched on SEO briefly in Chapter 4. Now, it's time to help you utilise its power and potential by focusing on the necessary elements needed to construct a successful SEO campaign. This will include a more detailed guide to keyword research to help you better understand this crucial part of promoting your website and its search ranking position.

What is Search Engine Optimisation (SEO)?

Firstly, it's essential to be able to accurately define what SEO is.

The term search engine optimisation stands for any kind of marketing carried out with the purpose of improving your Search Engine Results Page (SERP) ranking in search engines – including Google, Bing, Yahoo and any others of the like. SEO involves using a range of tactics and techniques to increase the number of visitors to a website, while focusing on growing visibility in organic (non-paid) search engine results. Search engine traffic can be split into two categories – organic traffic and paid traffic. We looked at paid traffic (PPC) in the previous chapter, which comes from the use of ads you would pay for on a per click basis. Organic traffic then, is the complete opposite. It is traffic that most of us will rely on as it's free traffic. Ensuring you gain the maximum advantage from it takes a lot of hard work through good SEO practice.

There are two forms of search engine optimisation: Onpage and Offpage. Onpage optimisation relates to the changes which you can make to your website and its content, designed around making it meet the criteria of a search engine's algorithm. The sole aim of such measures is to improve your website's position in the search rankings. If you've ever wondered why your website isn't showing up on the first page of Google, it's likely the content is lacking in the SEO department. There could be a bunch of onpage optimisation factors that need improving but some examples include; title optimisation, meta tags, HTML tags, images and keyword optimisation. We'll look at some of these in more detail shortly.

Conversely, offpage optimisation relates to bringing in external links from outside of your website. You can think of these working like an endorsement or review. They are basically other external sources linking back to your website giving it greater credibility in Google's opinion. External links can be from social media platforms too, not just other websites. Generally, the more recognisable and high authority links you can get back to your site, the more SEO juice you will have, meaning your chances of rising up the Google ranks in the search engine will increase significantly. Again, we'll look at external links in detail further on in the chapter.

Your onpage and offpage SEO only make up a part of how your overall search engine ranking is determined. In total, there are over 200 different ranking factors in Google's algorithm, or so the Google myth goes. I don't think anyone really knows the complete answer to this. Google changes its search algorithm around 500-600 times each year, many are minor, but some have a major impact on search results. It's hard to know what all the variables are and virtually impossible to optimise for all of them.

Your goal is to ensure you are naturally appearing as highly as possible on the search engine listings. You'll know yourself how far down a list you are likely to read; I personally tend not to look beyond the first page unless I really need to. In fact, did you know that, according to Chitika, 92% of people don't go beyond the first page of Google's search results? Though this statistic tends to fluctuate, it doesn't change too much year on year. Just ask yourself, how often do you really click forward to the next page when searching for something on Google?

Your accounting firm then, cannot afford to linger too far down the page. In a services industry, you will find that ranking too low will mean it's nigh on impossible to get spotted. If you would like to get around this problem, you need to re-build your entire website and marketing campaign strategy to pair up with what the search engines ask for.

And that is the hardest part: knowing what the search engines ask for. Speak to two different SEO consultants, and they'll give you two differing answers. What one expert sees as your ideal pathway, another will totally rule out. Add in the fact that search engines change rules and regulations all the time, and every search engine has its own criteria, you'll soon discover mastering SEO is a very hard thing to do.

You may be wondering why you should even bother at this point. Let me show you why SEO is so important.

Why do You Need SEO?

I get asked this quite often. For one thing, you need SEO because, if implemented correctly, it can make your website rank higher than the rest of the competition. When someone receives a list of search results to a keyword search, they will only look so far down the page before going with one of the available options presented to them. Given that the top result on Google tends to bring in around one third of all clicks, it's only natural you'll want to get your firm's website ranking at the top spot for relevant and specific keywords. I spoke about keywords earlier and will dig deeper into this shortly.

Given that approximately 50% of all clicks in total go to the first two results on Google, you absolutely need to aim to fall at the very least in third place. The further down your website appears in the search results the less chance there is of traffic being directed your way. Therefore, you should concentrate your efforts on at least appearing in the first half of search results on Page 1 of Google, ideally one of the top 3 spots to get some serious traffic to your site.

Why you need SEO goes beyond just lead generation though, you need SEO because it's about empowering your reputation. If you are the first or second pick on Google, you are perceived as being better to a prospective client than if you appear at the bottom of the page.

For SEO, you have to be ready to commit both time and money to make the process work. With so many factors at play, it takes patience to see results. When done correctly though, the results can be consistent *and* considerable. The main investment is your time, or the comparatively smaller fees for bringing in a consultant. For now, let's concentrate on making sure you can offer both a high-quality website with rich content and one that ranks well. This means every element of your website and content should be reviewed to ensure it gains points to add to your search engine ranking, without detracting from its appeal to visitors.

After all, what good is a highly optimised site if the content within it does not inspire the reader?

Let's look at establishing a clear plan of action for your SEO strategy.

How to Put in Place the Pillars of Quality SEO

Now it's time to determine the elements required to ensure you have a strong, cohesive SEO strategy. This can be broken down into three major pillars or categories:

1. Keyword Research
2. Onpage Optimisation
3. Offpage Optimisation

These three categories mark the single most important changes that you could make to your SEO efforts, in order for you to maximise results. They are the cornerstones of good optimisation. I'll break down **what** each of these are, **why** you need them, and **how** to best implement them.

Google uses software or internet bots known as 'crawlers' which are designed to systematically browse websites and pages all over the web. They look to determine the quality and relevancy of a website, including keyword usage and several other ranking factors. By using patterns to hunt down websites based on their language and phraseology in conjunction with keywords of a search query, these 'crawlers' help Google's algorithm to allocate the rank position for a webpage.

While there are many other factors which can determine your ranking, from the kind of links you have with reputable websites coming back to you (backlinks), through to the website layout or load speed, good optimisation is the primary concern.

For now, just take the time to read over those three key categories again. These will become the hallmark of your firm's website for years to come, so getting to grips with them right away is fundamental. It will take practice, testing and reviewing to get right over time. The pillars of a good SEO strategy are not something you can implement today and see instant results from tomorrow.

SEO is a long-term strategy. It needs constant work and refinement. Your optimisation strategy will need to grow and adjust to fit with modern SEO best practice and perpetual changes made to Google's algorithm. Done right, SEO is one of the strongest forms of naturally developed marketing around. It's putting in place a system that stops your website being lost in the vastness of the internet. It's one of your most powerful marketing tools out there.

So where should you start?

Keyword Research

First off, you should look to **establish the keywords your website needs to reach your target client.** Keyword research is at the heart of all SEO activities. Before you pick a single keyword to start working on, let me make one thing clear: there is such a thing as being too optimised.

If you were an internet user in the 1990s and early 2000s, you'll remember a sea of solid-colour websites loaded with keywords. These words were often just repeated in small boxes or hidden away behind images and the like. Today, such repetition would cause your website to move down in the rankings, not up. Using the same keywords and phrasing extensively and artificially without a natural flow is known as 'keyword stuffing' and it's something you must absolutely avoid.

Whatever keyword you are trying to rank for, you will have to make sure you use it naturally. The simplest way to know you managed this is to read the content back to yourself. As you do this ask yourself, would you use the same phrasing if you were you to speak the words out aloud? If the answer is no, then you should probably cut back on it!

The reason why you need to be so careful with optimisation and the selection of keywords is simple. Google and other search engines want pages to be relevant in **what they say**, not **what they rank for**. If your website is going to rank highly for the search terms you care about, then keywords must be:

a) relevant to the context, and,

b) used naturally.

There are some plugin tools and apps at your beck and call to help you with this. I'd recommend using Yoast SEO.

How to Pick the Right Keywords

The first major challenge you have when it comes to learning how to use keywords properly, is getting to grips with how to carry out keyword research. There is no universal, 100% proven way to pick keywords. Read one guide and the advice will vary wildly from the next. Typically, everything from your website size to your marketing budget, through to your competition and your ideal client profile, will all determine the keywords which you are looking for.

I spoke about picking the right keywords in Chapter 6, but for now it's important to work on expanding your keyword research further based on the following criteria:

- Start off by creating a series of keywords which will be known as your 'seed keywords', or the keywords that you want to target the most. They are defined by what your business is, and who your business is for. As an accountant, this should be built around the key services you wish to push.
- Next, you should see how your firm already fares on Google. To do this, head into your Google Search Console dashboard (run a simple Google search). This will show you what kind of keywords you are ranking for, what position you hold for each keyword and how well that keyword is doing for you.

- You may notice you are ranking in one way or another for hundreds of different keywords, maybe even thousands. You can then break this listing down to pick out 4-5 top performing keywords, and work towards maximising these in your website's main content. Other high performing keywords on the list may give you ideas for your blog content.
- Lastly, start using the Google Keyword Planner tool we looked at in Chapter 6. Use it *all* the time. Enter in search phrases based on the key problems your ideal client might have. Simply start adding 5-10 keyword phrases into the planner and see what kind of results come up. As you become more experienced with SEO, you can start using some more advanced tools, such as Market Samurai for identifying keywords which are particularly relevant to you, as well as many other useful metrics. In the beginning though, I'd suggest sticking to the Google Keyword Planner.

If the searches for one particular keyword are over 1000 per month and competition is not too high, you could consider these as alternative words to rank for. Ideally you want to try and choose keywords which have a high search volume but low competition. Going for high search volume and high competition keywords means you are tangling with very challenging ones to gain position. It's better to target those low-hanging fruits which you can realistically work towards ranking for at the top of the search engine listings.

With that in mind, it's essential you consider that location is often used as part of a search query, so you should include your address and relevant place names in full. For example, if you are an accountant in London, you'd often refer to yourself as being based in a particular area of the city. London, like any capital city, is massive; it would be very hard to rank for something like 'accountant London' due to the high volume of competition this would attract. Instead, ranking for 'accountant Stratford' or 'accountant Hammersmith', using your nearby locality is going to give you more chance of a good positioning for related search queries.

Keep that in mind no matter what city you are based in. Trying to rank high for the city alone (or at least having it as your primary keyword), is going to be difficult.

Now that you, hopefully, understand a bit more about trying to find good keywords to rank for, let's look at optimising the rest of your website to match up with your searches.

Onpage Optimisation

Once you have selected your keywords, it's important to work out how to go about fitting them in. Onpage optimisation is literally taking the keywords you came up with in the last section and using them naturally and routinely throughout your website content.

What onpage optimisation will do is make your website more relevant in the eyes of Google. Instead of just seeing the keyword repeated time and time again, search engines will consider your keywords' relevance to its context. It will pick up on the regular mixture of your content, ensuring it all matches up with the use of the keywords. Onpage optimisation speaks to the search engine crawlers, telling them you are a suitable pick as your website matches up to the search query, ticking the criteria boxes for the algorithm.

This should then explain why onpage optimisation is key to increasing your site visibility. Put simply, your website will not be able to bring you as much traffic without onpage optimisation. At the same time, optimising your website means that it will **literally read better to your ideal client**. It will appear more tailored to their interests, as the topics and writing will all be focused around the very issues they find important! They'll find your site to be a good source of quality information and a resource they can come back to when they need advice.

So how do you go about implementing onpage optimisation properly? What are the major changes that you should make onsite?

Page Titles and Heading Tags

First off, you can work on improving Page Titles and Heading Tags. This is relatively easy to do, though it might take some trial and error.

I recommend making the Page Title as search engine and keyword heavy as possible. For example, this could include something like: 'Making Tax Digital for VAT' or 'Not for Profits – Charities and CASCs'. Simple, strong, hits the target and makes it immediately obvious that you may just be what a potential client is looking for.

Your Page Titles and Heading Tags should use the 'headline' formatting style which works with the analytic tools provided by your content management system. If you are looking at the coding of your website, it should say <h1> THE TEXT </h1>.

Of course, the 1 in <h1> could change. H1 is often seen as your primary heading, the title of the page. H2 would be used for subcategories, and H3, H4 and so on would be subcategories within each other. Think of it like having a table of contents which reads '1''1.1''1.1.1' and so on. Header tags are just like these table categories.

These are standout points of the content. They draw the attention of the reader and make it easy for them to know what the section to come will cover. Using your keywords in these naturally will always be useful. It can be quite confusing at first, but you should be able to get your head around using Page Titles and Heading Tags to break up a page, with the smart use of keywords as part of this. Look at Fig. 7.1 below, which shows an example of Page Titles based on the keyword search term 'tax tips for directors' and how they are displayed in the Search Engine Results Pages (SERPs).

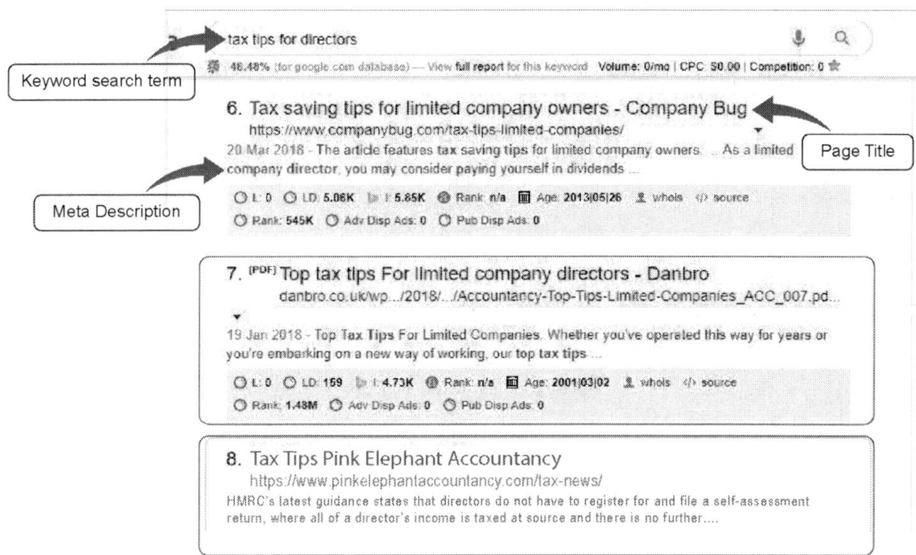

Figure 7.1

The above is a good example of the results that you would get from conducting a simple search for 'tax tips for directors'.

As you can see, there are three results that have come up on Google's first page. Which one of these would you be likely to click on? They are all relevant, but one particular firm of accountants here would get my vote. Hopefully you'll have guessed right? ... Indeed, it would be Danbro.

If I was a company director looking for tax tips, the first two results would have immediately got my attention because the Page Title displayed is descriptive and specific to what I need. The title for Pink Elephant Accountancy, at least from an SEO perspective, would have failed to capture my interest due to the lack of a keyword optimised Page Title. Although the article was in fact very valuable, having inspected it afterward, from an initial perspective it's not great for SEO.

'Tax tips' is a broad category and so I would immediately dismiss the idea of clicking through to Pink Elephant Accountancy's website, assuming that their information is not likely to be as good as Danbro or even Company Bug (who are already pulling me in due to a better Page Title). This is how most people browse and decide on how to shortlist their choices, so in this case it's quite an easy choice. Note, the listing appearing for Danbro is a PDF document which Google is picking up from the relevant page somewhere on Danbro's website, which draws my interest. This suggests it will be a valuable resource in the form of a document, which I could later end up sharing with others if I so wished.

Though the URL could do with some restructuring on their WordPress platform, the Meta Description is also a lot better than Pink Elephant Accountancy's. A Meta Description is the text snippet shown beneath the Page Title which describes the page in a bit more detail. It should always be equally as compelling and make use of the primary keywords.

If you're wondering what the metrics are that appear beneath each search result, this is just additional information provided by a useful SEO metric tool called SEOquake. I use this plugin occasionally to help me verify specific pages. Don't worry about this too much, but if you would like to play around with SEOquake you can download it for free and clip it on to your browser.

NICK'S TIPS

You can use tools like Yoast SEO and All in One SEO to customise the Page Titles and Meta Descriptions of your choice. This way your listing is displayed in Google exactly how you want it to, as opposed to Google making the choice for you. Plugin tools like this can make all the difference for potentially ranking your website above those of your competitors.

Headlines, Images and Body Text

While you should look to use your keywords within the headlines of your website, keywords also need to be added in naturally to the actual body of text and on your images. I don't mean actually writing them on the image but rather adding the image tag as a keyword. Your image tag is the text which appears if you highlight or inspect an image.

Search engines cannot read what an image is, they have no eyes, so to speak. They need to know how to interpret an image, thus a descriptive tag linked to the image enables 'web crawlers' to identify and recognise the image(s). Using a keyword in the descriptive tag helps an image to both rank better onsite and ensure the search engine understands the link. Why this is important should be obvious: it allows another use of your keyword whilst improving onsite optimisation. This is known as your 'alt' text and will be used as the placeholder if your image cannot load for whatever reason. Make sure the image is uploaded to the website with a name that makes sense, too. Uploading 'SA100-12434.png' is nowhere near as SEO-friendly as having the original file named as 'SA100 Tax Return 2019.png'. It's often the smallest things that make the biggest difference. In terms of how you do this, it's easy to change or update a tag, especially with WordPress. When uploading an image to your post or page, you can simply add in alt tags using the WordPress wizard.

Using your keywords naturally as you go within the body text makes it more attractive to Google, but this should be done with restraint. There should be some flow to the writing, so it doesn't detract from a reader's engagement. Again, think how it sounds if you read the article or content out loud to yourself or someone else. If it sounds like there is an excessive use of the keyword(s) within a paragraph, it's likely to be too much. Yoast SEO is a fantastic tool to help with this and can indicate whether content is too thin, as well as the keyword density. I would suggest installing this plugin in WordPress to help you assess your own SEO score.

URL Structuring

Another part of your onsite optimisation is going to be the selection of your site's page address protocol, the Uniform Resource Locator, commonly shortened to URL. A URL allows for better navigation by search engines, creating shortcuts to move a user directly to the page requested when pasted into a search bar or from a hyperlink. You may be wondering if a URL is the same thing as a domain name. It's a good question so let me demystify this for you with a simple non-technical explanation. A domain name is the actual name of the website while a URL may be any one of the pages within the domain. For example, the domain name for Pink Elephant Accountancy could be pinkelephantaccountancy.co.uk or pinkelephantaccountancy.com (no one really uses 'www.' anymore as it's not often required for searching or calling up a website or page). A URL is usually made up of several parts and points to a place within the site or specific page such as https://www.pinkelephantaccountancy.com/services/taxreturns.

You should always look to structure and optimise each onsite URL. You can define the URL to better fit with the message you wish to convey about its content or purpose. When it comes to your website, your URLs are often the first thing Google and users will see. Therefore, structuring your site's page address correctly and integrating your keywords when possible can help you score some great points when it comes to SEO.

It's important to ensure your website structure and hierarchy is correct and logically takes your visitors to their desired destination. Keeping this as simple as you can will not only ensure you benefit from SEO in the long-run but will also keep your visitors happy by providing better user flow and interaction. I have seen many sites where it takes a long time to figure out where to find the relevant information. This often results in a poor user experience and high bounce rates (visitors abandoning the site and going elsewhere).

With the example above, the URL for Pink Elephant Accountancy is a standard structure and is a pretty good way of doing it. It's clear to both Google and the user what this specific page is: https://www.pinkelephantaccountancy.com/services/taxreturns. There are two layers here, the main Services page and a secondary or subpage for Tax Returns. It's easy to follow and understand by anyone looking for this service. So, keep your layers to two or three to avoid users having to wade through irrelevant parts to get to the section they need, consequently affecting your site metrics.

Be sure to also take advantage of your keywords here too and integrate them into the page URLs. The keywords used should relate to what is on the page, hopefully with the natural use of a keyword within that URL. It's always better not to leave your URLs basic, generic or out of sync with the content on the page, as this will only hamper your success with SEO ranking later. Most content management systems will spit out a standard format for your URLs but you should customise these for a more logical user flow and include your keywords.

The reason for this is because you'll want your pages to be discovered by people (and crawlers) searching for related key terms. For example, if there are a lot of searches for 'filing tax returns', or 'preparing tax returns' or 'filing VAT returns' you could include the keywords in the URLs as well as the Page Titles. For Pink Elephant Accountancy, though the URL is absolutely fine and most businesses will have a similar structure with Services as the main layer, the subpages should be optimised here. Rather than having a broad search term like 'Tax Returns', you could have something like 'Preparing CIS returns' or 'Filing Corporation Tax returns' or 'Filing VAT returns'. This will avoid visitors taking a scenic route, getting lost on the way and lets them reach their desired destination quickly. It reduces your bounce rates and provides a better overall user experience.

Page Speed

Page speed or 'page load time' is how responsive the website or a specific page is to a search link, that is how much time it takes to load and fully display the content. When someone clicks on a link to your website, they expect it to appear in full in a few short seconds. For a professional firm's website, this shouldn't be too challenging, as it's probably relatively light in terms of imagery and other time consuming, load-heavy features.

The reason why page speed is an important part of optimisation is that, put simply, it's a major determining factor of rankings. Statistics show that users will click away if a page takes longer than five seconds to load. It doesn't matter if your site is at fault or if it's due to a poor internet connection. The sheer wealth of competition means visitors won't wait around. Unfortunately, being the very busy creatures that we are, we simply don't have much time to waste. In fact, we are often looking for excuses like this to help make our buying decisions easier. So, don't give a potential lead the easy excuse to move on to one of your competitors. If you don't do everything possible to improve and stabilise page load times, you are literally going to turn prospects away needlessly.

To know how well your website is loading, you can turn to the Google Page Speed Tool. This is easy to use; all you do is type in the URL of your website, and it will determine how good or bad load times are. **Don't disregard load times.** Correcting them can be quite an abstract experience as this may require anything from adjusting the format of your images to moving to a new hosting company altogether.

Google considers page load times among its most important criteria for your site's ranking, so make sure you do everything you can to improve loading speeds. It's good practice to stress test your own site from time to time, ensuring it stays responsive to any platform updates.

Offpage Optimisation

By the same token, you need to pay attention to the offsite elements of your online business presence. Optimisation does not just stop at making the actual website look good and perform better. Making sure that all associated tools, such as social media pages and landing pages outside of the main website are running well and follow the above onpage practices is equally important. More critical though, is to ensure you pay attention to the quality of links that come back to your website. These are known as **backlinks**.

They are links which come to your website from other websites and sources. Good backlinks help build up a lot of credibility for your website and encourage traffic which, in turn, adds to a positive SEO score for your website. The more prestigious or reputed the link coming back to your website, the better. For an accountancy firm, this could include links from relevant professional bodies and publications such as ACCA or AccountingWEB linking back to your website. Look at Fig. 7.2 below to give yourself an idea of how your site can receive inbound links from various sources.

Your website will be given a general score by Google that brings all your attributes and optimisation together. This score is known as your PageRank, and it's essential this is made as high as possible to achieve long-term success for your firm's website. Your site will start with a PageRank of 0, on the basis that it has no influence whatsoever. Major players in the online sphere, such as Google, hold the highest attainable PageRank of 10.

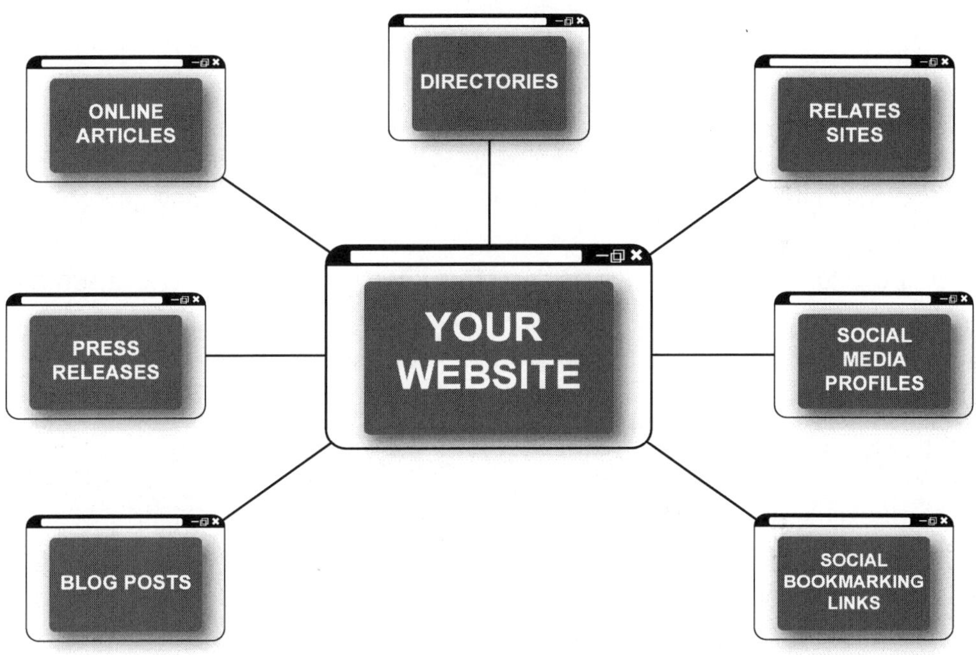

Figure 7.2

Why Offpage Optimisation is So Important

The reason why offpage optimisation matters is because **you could do every part of your onpage optimisation perfectly, and barely break into the first page of Google's listings from that alone.**

Offpage optimisation is what Google cares about. Generally, consider targeting professional bodies, reputable media sites and other connections related to your industry. This is not to say you should adopt the 'Any PR is good PR' strategy and go create a local scandal to get links from major news websites!

Speaking of avoiding bad PR, make sure you maintain a 'white hat' approach to SEO. This means that you use legitimate, honest tactics to get your website ranking up the search engines. Some sites resort to 'black hat' techniques, which are often likely to cause a spike in traffic but usually come with a penalty long-term. Not only that, but such techniques could become problematic from a reputational standpoint. At the very least, it can be hard to recover the stained reputation of a website with a history of black hat SEO techniques.

I have heard of some cases where companies used some freelancer sites for their backlinking activities, resulting in their websites getting blacklisted by Google as a consequence. So, while it's fine to outsource your backlink building activities, which I do recommend, be sure to choose a reputable agency for this. The long-term benefits will outweigh the costs, making sure you have a prestigious website which sits on solid foundations. Black hat techniques might deliver short-term results at a low cost but go against SEO best practice.

Each backlink you get will act as an endorsement for your company. And, just like getting an endorsement from a celebrity or an influencer, the more reputable the source, the more impact it will have. You would get far more benefit from a single PageRank 7 or 8 website linking to you than tens or even hundreds of PageRank 1 websites. Quality over quantity is certainly the case here.

The top sites ranking for the keywords you wish to do well in will likely achieve this thanks to offpage optimisation. How then can you acquire some authoritative and impressive links?

Using Backlinks to Your Advantage

The solution to this is amazingly simple: you have to find out who is providing backlinks to those above you in the search results. Try to arrange a similar reciprocal link to your website from those providers. You can use a backlink checker tool such as the wonderfully named Backlink Watch to reverse trace your competitors' backlinks.

Type in the website address of your top ranked competitor, and then hit the 'Check Backlinks' button and let the tracer do its magic. While it might take some time, it will give you a clear idea of who is helping your competitors get to the top and who is most influential in their rise. Then, you simply need to contact these organisations and try to get a similar link from them back to your site. Simple right?

A good way to build up strong and immediate offpage optimisation is to do the following:

- Create **social media profiles** for your firm on all the major social media platforms. I'll talk about these a bit later, but a link back from your social media profile is a good start.
- Find any and all **local, regional and national business directories.** Some are free to sign up to while others may ask for a subscription. Sign up to as many as you can, create a profile on each and complete it with unique content which includes a link back to your site.
- Contact recognised media sites or high-profile blog writers and blog site hosts that include content related to your industry, e.g. AccountingWEB, ACCA, Medium. Speak to them about the possibility of creating a guest post on their behalf, written by you, with a link to your site.
- Provide a backlink strategy, linking to their website in return for them doing the same for you. This could go on a section of your site titled 'Recommended Reading' or you could simply embed the hyperlinks within the body text of your content. It would very much depend on the style and theme of your website. I suggest you be proactive and include a link to their site prior to contacting them, showing commitment to any potential partnership.

Always try to ensure that the link is using a keyword for your website, too. Simply saying 'click here', or something similar, could leave you locked into any other link on the web which also says, 'click here', and think how many of them exist!

Lastly, you will have to show some patience as backlinks won't deliver changes overnight. Like any other part of SEO, offpage elements take a winding route to high ranking scores which is just something you'll need to get used to. The long-term results, though, alongside quality onpage optimisation, will be more than worth it.

Now that you can appreciate the art of building an optimised and secure website with solid foundations and strong supporting structures, it's time to move on to your next most important tool: **the long-term, beneficial power of Google My Business, online listings and review sites which can enhance both your SEO and your reputation.**

Takeaways

- You need to be ready to make serious changes to your website, and your supporting pages on the internet, if you wish to bring in more traffic.
- Check your keyword choices to determine the best way to use these in relation to targeting your ideal client. Then ensure they are inserted into your content naturally.
- Work on both onpage and offpage optimisation or it may be a painful experience in achieving real results for your business website, so make both a priority.
- Creating backlinks to your website is essential, as links from other influential sources act as endorsements for yours.
- Make sure any backlinking activities which you outsource come from an agency who you can trust to do so by ethical means.
- The goal of all SEO is to rise up the SERPs for search engine recognition, be aware that these can change from engine to engine and over time. There isn't one single solution to all.

CHAPTER 8

GOOGLE MY BUSINESS, LISTINGS & REVIEWS

The previous chapter addressed the need for both onpage and offpage optimisation for your website. It's essential that your website and all your online pages are speaking in the same voice and style. With these fundamentals in place, it's time to start working on another piece of the puzzle: **reputation management**.

As a professional your reputation goes a long way towards your success. It's that simple. I recommend you spend some time getting to grips with using the following: Google My Business, Directory Listings and Reviews.

All three of these online tools help to characterise your business in so many ways. With that in mind, you must absolutely learn how to use each of these tools to your advantage. Alongside being crucial to your SEO, they will play a leading role in your overall reputation as a business. In the professional services industry, the feedback other people leave about your work is vital to growing trust in the firm and attracting new clients.

So, how can you ensure your business is being seen in the right light? With 90% of your potential clients reading online reviews before they consider engaging a professional, how you come across online has never had greater impact.

Let's begin by looking at the first tool: Google My Business. This is an extremely useful piece of kit to have in your arsenal and, luckily for you, it's vastly underutilised in the professional services industry.

What is Google My Business?

It's a directory-like solution that Google came up with. It was once known as Google Places, but is now known as Google My Business, or GMB.

This is a popular source for locating or researching a business today, especially for those in need of professional services. It's a powerful solution that gives you a way to control your business presence online. It's also great for making sure you appear more reliably on Google searches, and on Google Maps.

It will help you to improve your business listing, standing and reputation – and it will provide a long-term, natural benefit to your search engine rankings. If you want to get started with Google My Business, you simply need to go to google.co.uk/business. You can sign up for free.

GMB is a chance to add some real-world validation to your business and more importantly, it's integral to your local search SEO. By using it, you will be able to increase your visibility and credibility in a very short space of time. This means that when people search for your business, or your primary keyword (e.g. accountant LOCATION), most of the time they will see a little Google Maps section onscreen showing where you are physically based with some general business details.

Let's look at a quick example to help demonstrate what I mean.

Say I'm searching for an accounting firm in West London, in the Kensington area, I can simply go to Google, or any other search engine, and type in the words 'accountant Kensington'. I've just done that now and look what comes up:

40% 19:28
ttps://www.google.com
3
Small Business Accountants | Low Monthly Fee | TheAccountancy.co.uk
Ad www.theaccountancy.co.uk/
Friendly And Business Accounting Services. Get An Instant Quote! Fixed monthly fees.
SHEPHERD'S BUSH
Flake & Co.
Buckingham Palace
Greenman Javis
KNIGHTSBRIDGE
HAMMERSMITH
Saatchi Gallery
Open now
Visited
Not visited
MORE FILTERS
Morgan Reach Chartered Accounta...
5.0 ★★★★★ (3)
Accountant · 239 Kensington High St
Closed · Opens 9AM Fri
CALL
Review Count
Flake & Co.
5.0 ★★★★★ (1)
Accountant · House 14, Partridge, 75 Ken...
Closed · Opens 9AM Fri
CALL
Greenman Javis
No reviews
Accountant · Mansion House, 38 Roches...
Closed · Opens 9:30AM Fri
CALL

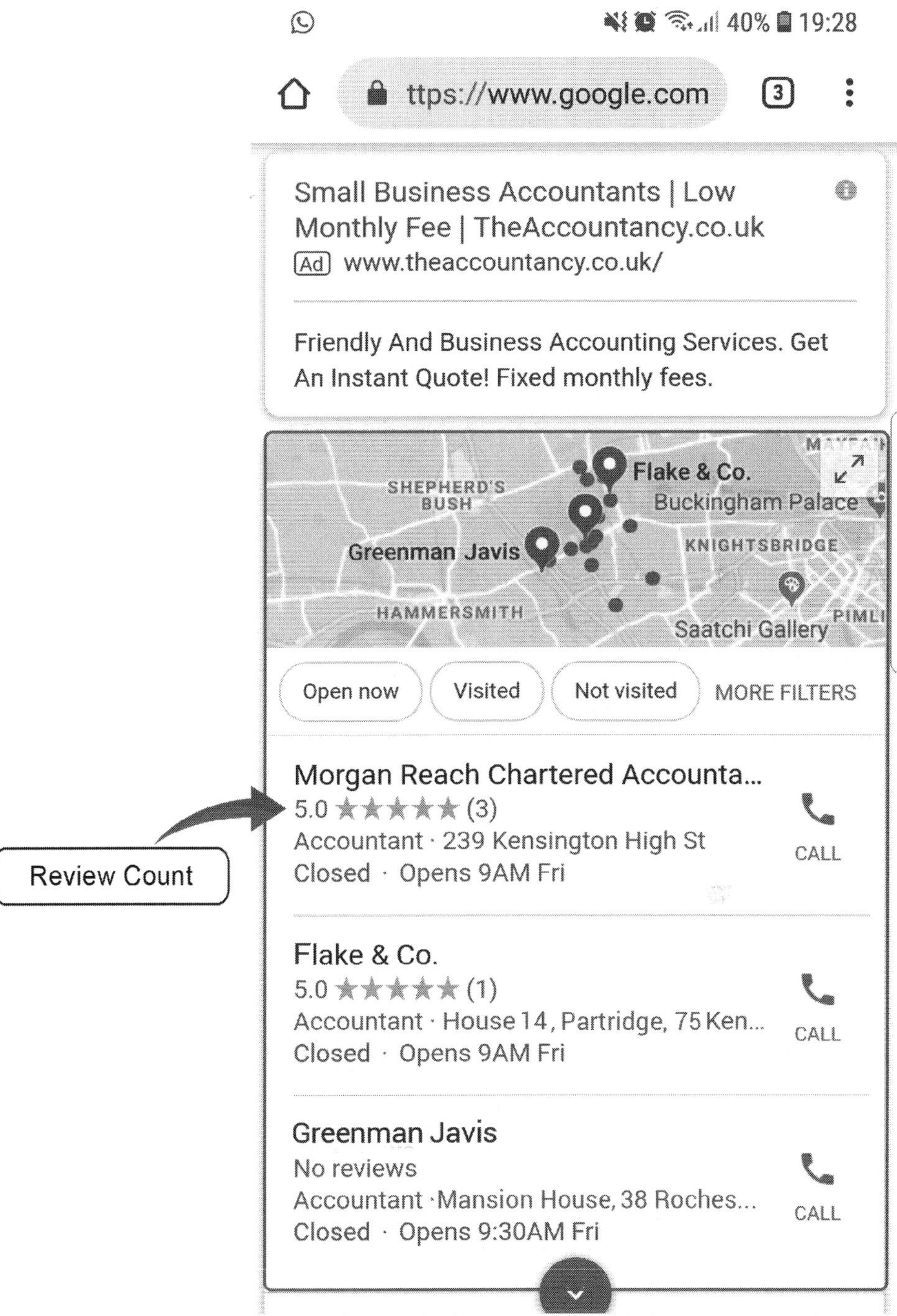

Figure 8.1

As you can see from Fig. 8.1, the top 3 firms that are visible in the Google search results have appeared instantaneously. These include Morgan Reach Chartered Accountants, Flake & Co and Greenman Javis. They are all marked on Google maps and shown directly below with some business information. The business address, contact information and map directions make it incredibly easy for people to immediately work out where businesses are based and get in touch within a couple of clicks. If we take it a step further and look at the reviews, you can immediately see Morgan Reach has three 5-star reviews, Flake & Co has one 5-star review and Greenman Javis has none.

As a potential prospect looking for an accounting firm, who do you think I would be inclined to call? The one with the most reviews, of course. Morgan Reach would be the clear winner here as they look like the most up-to-date and active accounting firm. Now they may not be the best possible firm out there, but the chances are they will be quite good as they are appearing in the number 1 spot.

So, there are two things to take away here. Firstly, if you don't have a GMB account you are massively missing out on potential business. Secondly, if you do have one, the chances are you aren't optimising it as well as you could be. In this example, Flake & Co and Greenman Javis may be just as good firms, if not better than, Morgan Reach. However, as they haven't fully optimised their GMB account and made use of reviews, they are not likely to get that enquiring phone call. Which we all want, right? Things like reviews play a large role in how we evaluate a potential business or service which we may consider using. It can often be the deciding factor when it comes to driving business. I'll cover reviews shortly.

EXERCISE 1

Type in the words 'accountant LOCATION' (where your firm is based) and see what comes up on Google. You can do this test for whatever profession you're in; legal, actuarial or otherwise. What position are you appearing in? If it's not in the top 3 spots, you may need to work on optimising your GMB account. If you're not appearing altogether, you should look to fix this right away.

Why You Need a Google My Business Account

It should be obvious why your business needs a GMB account, giving you greater visibility and validation. It immediately removes any doubt that you are a fictional or fly-by-night company. Add in the fact that the PageRank of GMB is huge, and you are able to easily boost offpage optimisation in a flash. This is, essentially, how many firms are found instantly, as could be seen from the example above**. If you aren't using Google My Business, you are missing out on a great opportunity to get noticed**. With four out of five prospective clients now conducting an online search prior to deciding who to purchase from, this is another platform where you can promote your services, display your credentials and gain visibility. With so many not making the most of Google My Business, you have ample opportunity to snap up much of the business your competition may be leaving behind!

For example, a client I recently worked with was doing quite well in the legal sector. However, they weren't using GMB at all. My team created a GMB account for them and optimised it based on the ideas covered in this book. After just two weeks? They'd moved up to second spot for local search options and brought in twelve new leads. That was a significant result!

As GMB is so closely tied in with Google Maps it enables you to promote your firm effectively to prospects in your catchment area. Google Maps is most commonly used on mobiles which is also the preferred device for sourcing many professional services. The combination of a visible location and the star rating of reviews can work very much in your favour when someone is looking to choose a firm. You'll have around 200 characters to sum up your business, so it's obviously a good time to use your keywords, again as naturally as possible. Your ideal client will feel much more comfortable getting in touch thanks to you having a verified GMB profile. You also gain greater online visibility. It's a win – win situation!

How to Create Your Google My Business Account

This is extremely easy, and really shouldn't take you very long at all. All that you need to do is the following:

1. Head over to the Google My Business page, found at google.com/business as above.

2. Once you are there, sign in. You ought to be able to do this with your standard Gmail account credentials.

3. On this page, click 'Start Now', which should be towards the top right-hand corner. Enter in the name of your business and hit 'Next'. Then, enter your business address. Choose whether you wish to show or hide your address, I'd recommend showing it. Click 'Next'.

4. Select your business category, add in your phone number and website, and then hit 'Next'.

5. Now, you will need to verify your business, which can be done through various methods. The most common choices will be either phone, email or by direct mail. Google will issue you a verification pin by text, email or postcard. You are then directed to an onscreen wizard which makes setting up your listing super simple.

Once you follow through with this, you have essentially created a verified account for your business. Now, you should look at how to improve the standing of your GMB profile. Let's consider best practice for a modern GMB listing for an accountancy firm.

Google My Business Best Practice

- Make sure you take the time to include factual details about your business. If you have won any awards, for example, make that clear in the description.
- Include both a primary keyword and your specialist service quality or attribute in your main GMB profile so your ideal client can immediately work out who you are and what you are about.
- Set major categories for your accountancy firm and ensure they are relevant to the skills you offer. If you don't want to be recognised for doing bookkeeping, don't select bookkeeping!
- Work out what catchment area you are happy to be seen within, as this will help you to ensure your listing only appears in location searches that are suitable and practical for you to target.
- In the 'Additional Details' section, be sure to include every service you offer: Prioritise your specialist skills but don't omit any additional areas that your firm can provide here.
- Keep checking in to update and improve your profile as much as you can. Putting up photos of your premises, and even your staff, can add an air of professionalism which may have been missing.

You need to try and stand out from the crowd around you. While it might not apply to your competition, many accountants don't make use of the Google My Business posts section. Be sure to fill this in with relevant information and useful shouts. It doesn't need to be done in the form of blog-style posts. Informative, short posts to keep people up-to-date with company changes can make a lot of sense and may even set you apart from the rest.

Many accountancy firms have a GMB account but do not use it to market themselves. You need to make your account distinctive, so do some research into those of your competition and look for a gap in how they portray themselves. Don't forget to get some reviews to give you that great 5-star rating. It will take some time and a bit of trial and error to find the GMB profile which best speaks to your clients, but it's very much worth it.

Finally, verify the listing and you should start seeing a set-in-stone GMB profile appear for your business, which only you are entitled to edit. It's easy, effective and notably among the more powerful offpage optimisation tools you can use.

Directory Listings

Now that you have filled out your Google My Business page, it's time to look at a similar profile for your firm in Directory Listings. If you are someone who grew up with the Yellow Pages, you'll know what a directory listing is; it's the online equivalent to this. Essentially, you provide basic details about your business to appear in local and national directory listings.

A directory listing is a location for people to search for the experts they need. From an accountant to a butcher, a carpenter to a plasterer, we use directory listings for all manner of reasons. What they tend to do though, is help us to find businesses which are:

a) local and

b) trusted.

Many local directories will exist in your area, whether you are based in Newcastle, Nottingham, London, Leeds, Grimsby or Glasgow. Everywhere in the United Kingdom has local online directories, many of which are free to use. **Each listing you fill in then, will contribute in some way towards building up your offsite optimisation**.

But why should you bother? Isn't Google simply stronger than all these directory sites put together?

Why You Need to Make the Most of Directory Listings

Put simply, more business listings will bring you more clicks. In fact, according to BrightLocal, around 25% of your customers will call after seeing one of your local business listings. They will be more likely to call, click or visit after coming across you in a local listing. With the opportunity to create so many listings then, rejecting the benefits they offer is foolish.

While I stressed importance of quality over quantity, the more online directory listings you have the better, especially for a professional firm. They are always seen as being applicable to your business niche, and the fact they draw so much traffic, even smaller directories, makes them a wonderful tool for SEO growth. Having a good number of listings means you can add a large collection of medium-to-high quality backlinks to your business website and social media accounts, generating leads and creating clients.

Another reason why you need to spread your net so wide is for maximum SEO impact. For example, you may find that your Google My Business listing draws in more traffic than any one of these directory listings will by itself. But each listing takes only a few minutes to create, a short period of time to optimise, and could generate you added traffic for free.

You will find that many smaller directory listings are frequently, in some way, tied in with the bigger directories. They might be used a lot of the time by smaller sites and businesses, so the visibility in local communities they offer is incredible. The simplest reason why you ought to create directory listing pages, is that it's so easy, you are literally rejecting free SEO benefits by not doing so!

Finding the Right Directories to Sign Up To

To start off with, you should look to create a directory listing on all or most of the following websites:

- Yell.com **www.yell.com**
- Yelp.co.uk **www.yelp.co.uk**

- Freeindex.co.uk **www.freeindex.co.uk**
- Business-directory-uk.co.uk **www.business-directory-uk.co.uk**
- Uksmallbusinessdirectory.co.uk **www.uksmallbusinessdirectory.co.uk**
- Thomsonlocal.com **www.thomsonlocal.com**
- Unbiased.co.uk **www.unbiased.co.uk**
- Xero.com **www.xero.com**
- Chekin.co.uk **https://chekin.co.uk**
- Accountant-directory.co.uk **www.accountant-directory.co.uk**
- The Legal 500 **www.legal500.com**
- The Modern House **www.themodernhouse.com**

Of course, not all these options will be right for you. Some simply might lack the reach you need, while others won't suit your professional practice. You will also have local options based on your office address, and for any branches you may have. Be sure to carry out some Google searches for terms like: 'business directories LOCATION' and 'accountancy directories LOCATION' and you should easily find some local choices.

Since many firms draw much of their clientele from their own community anyway, it makes sense to draw in some positive responses to your business from your local directories. How then, can you go about making sure you have quality directory listings?

Optimising Your Directory Listings

The way you create your directory listings will vary from site to site. Most of the time, you will fill in much the same information as you provided for Google My Business; business name, address, industry, specialist skills, imagery and contact details. The sheer number of listings which I come across that aren't close to being optimised, even without making the most of reviews, is staggering. Just like your GMB account, each listing must be properly optimised to get the best possible results.

To help you avoid issues with SEO and to get as many hits as you can from each listing, I'd recommend sticking to the following:

- Make sure each business listing is unique and makes use, naturally, of your primary keyword. They might say similar things, but they should each be written a little differently from one another.
- Creating an instant personal connection is essential. It's why I recommend you highlight the key decision maker(s) within your firm by name to foster trust.
- Try and include your specialist services in the form of a Call-to-Action on any business directory, too. It should advertise your best skills and encourage the reader to click.
- Always make that Call-to-Action stand out, try and deliver it as close to the top of your body text in the listing for maximum impact.
- Leave an actual contact address. Only linking to a contact form can feel impersonal, so provide a less generic contact method which tells them who they are calling or getting in touch with.
- If the business directory offers the opportunity to collect reviews (see below), then be sure to actively encourage that within the business directory writing.
- Ensure every directory matches to the same overall image of your business, albeit in a different way. Try different target styles and/or answering different questions on each directory, using variations on the same theme and message.

If you do all the above, you will be much more likely to create enticing and professional directory listings which do the job you want them to. Now you know what a directory listing is, why it's important, and how to set each one up to maximum benefit, let's look at reviews.

Reviews

You need to ensure you make positive use of and monitor online reviews. A review is a client-created commentary or feedback about what **your business has done for them.** As an accountant, it's important you encourage clients to leave reviews which entice other potential ideal clients to pick up the phone.

Put simply, the importance of high-quality reviews cannot be overstated. It's how we choose many of our services, and it's no different when choosing a professional service provider, in fact it can be the deciding factor. Individuals will happily carry out a quick Google search and either use a search result or a directory listing site such as those above to pick out their chosen professional.

Therefore, you need to be ready to stand out as the best choice in your local area. To do that, you have to demonstrate where you've helped others previously by solving their problems and adding value. The surest way to demonstrate this, of course, is with reviews.

The voice of your consumer is so important, and a high-quality review will do so much for your reputation, and for your offsite optimisation. Google loves being able to give the voice back to the people, and this is one of the reasons why you **need to take so much care with the use of reviews.**

Why Reviews are Your Most Powerful Currency

Did you know that reviews are your most valuable currency in terms of reputation management and first-impression building with your ideal client?

If someone were to post a negative review of your business on Google, YouTube or anywhere else, the stain could be very hard to remove. Sadly, the society we live in today gives more weight to a negative experience than a positive one. You have 50 reviews, and only one of them is a negative: which do you think stays in the mind of the reader?

Therefore, reviews are your most powerful currency. With around nine-tenths of all consumers turning to an online review before moving forward, you cannot afford to ignore their relevance. Remember that reviews are often the final deciding factor in favouring one particular business, as you saw from Morgan Reach in the earlier example.

If two firms look to be equal in quality, then the review count might just be what tips the scales. If people are willing to run through reviews of a £20 pair of shoes or a £10 meal, you can safely say that they'll investigate how your firm can help them out too!

People will naturally go for the firm which displays the highest quantity of good recommendations. You would probably do the same yourself. Positive public opinion is hard to earn. So, when we see other individuals earnestly promoting a business, it makes us eager to find out why.

Add on the fact that reviews are such a powerful solution for SEO, due to their organic nature and the way platforms take account of such feedback, it's a no-brainer to really push reviews as a major part of your marketing structure. How then, can you go about doing this properly? Let's look at putting in motion a professional way to build up your reviews.

EXERCISE 2

Head on over to Google and carry out a search on your business feedback. Look at what your own review score is. If you have any reviews from clients, see what they have written about you and now compare it to those of your competitors. Then contact 3 of your clients and ask them for a review. You could potentially outrank your competitors by completing this one simple task!

Creating a Professional Review Structure

While there are some things you can do to help improve your review process, the first thing you should concentrate on is doing it organically. Persuading clients to leave reviews will become easier if you make the process itself simpler. You also just need to concentrate on doing the best job possible for each and every client.

If you feel confident enough that you've done a stellar job for a client, you could ask them to leave a review for you. Incentives should never be offered for a good review though, only a genuine one can foster long-term trust and loyalty. If a client is appreciative in their praise of the job which you have done, ask them to leave a review on Google My Business, your social media pages etc. The greater the reviews, the greater your firm's reputation will be.

Remember, try to share reviews wherever your firm has an online presence, including your own website if a review system is set up there. The more platforms that carry reviews of your work, the more pages you are pulling a positive PageRank benefit from. It's better to have 25 reviews split across 10 platforms than having too many reviews displayed on any one site.

If you have a few reviews included on each platform or listing, then this all adds to your credibility across the board. The easier you make the feedback process, the more likely you are to see reviews being left. There's still more you can do to improve your ratings but concentrating on the above to begin with will really help you out later on.

Dealing with a Challenging Client in the Review Process

Of course, if you are dealing with a client who is annoyed and needs you to do more, or is threatening to disparage your business, you must quickly react and set in stone a plan to help solve their problem.

Considering the impact of negative reviews can quite easily drive away 40% of potential customers, according to a BrightLocal survey, dealing with negative reviews and disgruntled clients is paramount. The best way to protect your online reputation is to anticipate and revise any potential negative feedback as early as possible.

There are many ways you can do this. If you are in a situation where a client has left a negative review you must respond promptly. The longer you leave it, the harder it will be to remove the stain from your firm's reputation. I would recommend taking the issue offline as soon as possible. Rather than replying to an adverse review, respond to the complaint/comment privately through email or phone.

You'll often find you are able to resolve matters much more easily by taking prompt action in a professional and discrete way. The position you really want to be in though, is having control measures in place to monitor your online presence and manage your reputation. Using reputation management tools can help you do this and prevent you from receiving a negative review in the first place.

For example, a client of mine, an accounting firm, almost lost approximately £8,000 worth of business from their existing clientele in January. The only way this was identified was due to the feedback given by their clients who were honest enough to leave a review for the firm sharing their concerns. We sent out automated emails prompting reviews as part of the reputation management service we offer.

Two clients reported they were not happy and were ready to look for another accounting firm as they could not get their accountant on the phone, despite having sent numerous emails. In fact, they had already begun to look around for alternatives in the area. Another thing to note here is that they were more than happy to voice their opinions about the firm, and let the world know about it on Google Reviews. It was vital we acted quickly to avoid it becoming a major issue.

Fortunately, we were able to protect my client from any negative publicity. From the reputation management software in place, we identified the concerned clients through their feedback, but more critically, managed and controlled the after effects by reacting to the situation quickly and efficiently. The software helped protect my client from any stains to their reputation by not displaying any negative reviews in the public domain, using a funnel process. Without getting too technical, how this works is by filtering - displaying only above average Google rating scores on Google Reviews and not those that are below average. Poor reviews are brought to management's attention via email. Quite a clever piece of software kit, right? It lets you show off your best reviews while discreetly giving you notice to act decisively on others.

Consequently, the partner of the firm was able to speak directly to the clients in question and was able to settle their issues and retain them. Had we not sent out the emails in the first place, this would most probably have gone the other way, resulting in a loss of revenue and a tarnished reputation for the firm.

This is the power of reputation management. If you can control and manage your clients and automate the process, it will only help your firm prosper in the long run.

My client sent me a box of chocolates and M&S vouchers to thank me for helping protect their firm's reputation and repairing their relationship with some of their clients. I think the key lesson here, is never assume you're doing an outstanding job for your clients. Managing and looking after hundreds, if not thousands of clients can be incredibly difficult, so if you are able to automate your reputation management, why wouldn't you?

NICK'S TIPS

A sneaky but useful tip for staying on top of your reviews, is by setting Google Alerts for things like 'BUSINESS NAME reviews'. By implementing a routine Google Alert for your firm you'll be notified whenever new reviews pop up online about you. You can set alerts for pretty much anything. This can also be used to help generate ideas of what content to include in your blog posts for example.

Now that you are in position where you appreciate the power of these three marketing tools to facilitate your firm's visibility and reputation, let's move on. It's time to start looking at how to get you some quality leads through my favourite platform: LinkedIn.

Takeaways

- Building and managing your online professional reputation is as crucial as optimising your website to gain the visibility you require to draw in your ideal client.
- Utilising the power of tools like Google My Business and online reviews are so important to present the right image for your business and attract prospective clients.
- You have to be ready to promote your online business presence and reputation wherever individuals might search for you, using tools like directory listings to further maximise your reach.
- Reviews are the lifeblood of a professional service business and doing all that you can to capture regular positive reviews is essential to your growth and development.
- Refreshing and monitoring your reviews by using reputation management software can help you to optimise and control them, thus protecting your firm's image and reputation.

CHAPTER 9

LEAD GENERATION THROUGH LINKEDIN

In the last chapter, I spoke about how using reviews can help increase your social influence and reach online. You learned how reviews, directory listings and the use of Google My Business can add to the visibility of your business online. You also learned how to use each of these tools to enhance your reputation and authority. Now, let's move on to looking at the next part of your marketing strategy in terms of lead generation through a powerful platform: **LinkedIn**.

This is my favourite platform and one I spend a lot of time on. For me, LinkedIn is the best tool available to gain quality leads and target ideal clients. I personally help my clients run progressive LinkedIn marketing campaigns on a regular basis. With that in mind, I want to break down some crucial elements of LinkedIn which you can benefit from.

It's a topic that I could write about at length, so I'll do my best to summarise the key points for you as succinctly as I can. Networking on LinkedIn is essential to your business growth and development. Regardless of what profession you are in, you'll find your ideal client waiting for you on LinkedIn. In fact, most of my clients are sourced via this platform. I will show you how to do this and discover quality leads to grow your business. But first you need to understand the fundamentals of the platform.

What is LinkedIn?

It's an online social/business network specifically aimed at business professionals. Whether you want to find a particular business to work with or for, network with others in your profession, find a freelance contractor or find an employee, LinkedIn is a fine place to start your search. It's for anyone who is looking for new opportunities in the world of business, giving access to key influencers and decision makers.

It's often referred to as the 'Facebook for professionals', but that's not an adequate description of what its design and purpose is. Think of LinkedIn instead as the biggest networking event in the world, with people from all types of businesses displaying their credentials and inviting you to contact them. It has around 560 million users spread across 200 countries, including 23 million users in the United Kingdom alone. It's easy to see why LinkedIn is so popular and growing rapidly, with two new members creating a LinkedIn account **every single second!**

Your personal profile can advertise all your specialist skills and experience, showcasing your professional suitability to meet the needs of your ideal client. It acts like a business card for members, inviting you to sort through and reach out to those who might want your help. Connecting to and communicating with individuals within the platform is easy. You can talk to members via the private messenger service, enabling you to open a dialogue with anyone who is active and online. Best of all? With millions of users checking their LinkedIn profile daily, this means you have access to hundreds of new leads and potential clients who are all actively engaging with the community.

The layout is user friendly and the features it offers are diverse and simple to get to grips with. Overall, it should become your most commonly used social media platform for both networking and marketing. I'll cover other social media tools to consider using in the next chapter, so don't worry about them for now.

Why do You Need LinkedIn?

You might be wondering why you even need to use LinkedIn in the first place? The answer to this question is straightforward. **The main reason why you should use LinkedIn is that it allows for easy direct marketing**

and networking to your ideal client. It also puts you in direct contact with the decision maker, not merely someone who could pass on your details. Liaising with key people directly works much better than communicating with them through an intermediary, such as a receptionist. I think we've all been there at some stage in our lives and it's frustrating to say the least. It's one of the main reasons I use LinkedIn regularly, to identify and contact decision makers. Why waste time when it's possible to cut straight through to the ones who matter most?

Since you are probably looking for professionals, LinkedIn is the natural place to start. The messages most members receive are of a business nature, and the main purpose for anyone to post on the platform is to showcase their professional skills to make relevant business connections.

No other social media platform makes it so convenient to directly target and connect with potential clients (including your ideal clients) as LinkedIn. It's built to deliver top quality networking opportunities, and since everyone on the site is a professional, you'll waste little time in speaking to the wrong person.

But with so many members, including your competitors, how do you get spotted on something so big? With over 562 million profiles, you have to stand out. Just like for the search engines, you need to have an optimised profile.

Optimising Your LinkedIn Profile

Before I go any further, it's critical to note that this is your PERSONAL LinkedIn profile. I get asked all the time whether a company page should take priority over a personal page? My answer is always the same. While it's useful to have a company page set up on LinkedIn, most people are not searching for your company details on this platform. **Therefore, the emphasis should primarily be on your personal page. People buy from people, they will search for *you* and want to connect with *you* to eventually do business with.**

So, if you want to use LinkedIn to your benefit, you have to appreciate its advantages and understand the protocols. Before you start building any kind of lead generation campaign though, you must first follow a process. **To begin this process you need to create a fantastic profile which jumps off the screen.** This is such a crucial part of using LinkedIn to your advantage. Unfortunately, many professionals leave much to be desired with their individual profiles.

I am about to show you why so many of your competitors might not appreciate what LinkedIn can do as a marketing tool. In general, they either don't understand the process or are using LinkedIn ineffectively without harnessing its full potential. If you get your profile right, you can create an immediate invitation for your ideal clients to get in touch, as well as the opportunity to highlight how you are able to help them out.

There are many things which you could do to optimise and improve your LinkedIn profile. To get you started, though, the fundamental steps I recommend have been broken down below. Your ideal client must see that you are both active and credible, so let's look at how to go about creating a high-quality LinkedIn profile.

Create a Clean, Crisp Headshot

To start out you should get a professional quality photo taken of you. This is central to your appeal as it shows you off in the right light. If you intend to make a positive first impression, your profile picture is a big part of achieving this. You can probably use a smartphone to do this, as most these days come with superb camera quality.

The image should be in focus, crisp and appealing, as you have to make a good impression from the outset. For a LinkedIn profile you want to portray yourself as competent, experienced and proficient. Don't be shy, give your biggest and best smile! Let your prospects know you are personable as well as professional. After all, we remember companies by the individuals we interact with.

Use Your Company Logo as the Cover Photo

Next, you should look to get a high-resolution vector of your company logo created. Getting a vector of the logo is important, as it can be stretched and adjusted in size without losing crispness or quality. This is practical to include as it helps to show interested viewers both who you are, and the company which you represent. It creates an association of the company with the expert they, hopefully, want to hire!

Create a Captivating Headline and Summary

Every good LinkedIn profile carries a well-optimised headline and summary section. Your headline is the most crucial part of your profile because it's the first thing anyone will see alongside your lovely smiley photo. In the headline, be sure to use at least one of the most common search terms for your main area of expertise so the LinkedIn algorithm finds you in response to those relevant search terms. I see so many profiles that are under-optimised, where they don't focus on using the right keywords, or the headline is just not compelling enough. If you're not doing this right, you're missing out on being found by your ideal clients and not attracting the right connections. Naturally, you want to ensure you reach as many prospects as possible.

For example, a client of mine, a VAT specialist, just had the word 'Director' in his headline. If someone is looking for a VAT specialist, using 'Director' as a primary keyword is not going to do much good. After all, the search algorithm for LinkedIn can only retrieve results based on keywords which closely match the search terms. Therefore, you need to be very specific in describing how you come across to prospects. After optimising his profile and using the keyword 'VAT expert' instead, his searches increased by 650%.

So, instead of using generic terms like 'Director' or 'Partner' think about your ideal clients and what keywords they would use to find the services they want. Use relevant keywords which people are likely to search for like 'Tax specialist', 'Tax expert', 'VAT specialist', 'VAT expert' and so on.

Then, follow the same process with your summary section. Think about your ideal client and try to speak to them directly. You should look to include natural use of your headline keyword, and another keyword of a similar style, to help speak to the client *and* improve your overall profile optimisation.

Try and think of how you wrote your website content. Think of the main problem that you wish to target and then ensure you acknowledge the problem *and* offer the solution. Remember, you have up to 2000 characters here to utilise, so be wise and make the most of your keywords to help the LinkedIn algorithm favour your profile over others for the terms you most want to be identified with.

Include an Experience Section

Before anyone will hire your professional expertise, they'll want to see what you have done so far to justify their selection. To support this, display your most current and recent experience first. Your previous experience does not have to be so comprehensively listed. What you were doing in 1995 might convey expertise to you, but most clients care about what you do today. Accountancy changes all the time. How you helped someone in a previous decade tells them little about what you are able to do for them in the present climate. This is a fine chance for you to showcase some much-needed expertise.

In terms of keyword optimisation, try and slip in your primary keywords when talking about each service you are offering. This is another great section for making the most of your keywords, just as in the summary section. So, if you worked for another firm until recently, helping clients with business advisory, you could include keywords like 'business advisory' or 'advisory services'. Whatever expertise you have to promote, include a relevant keyword in each description.

Showcase Your Skills and Endorsements

You want to make use of this section well, as it shows others what you are able to do for them. Sure, they know you are an accountant but that can mean a lot of things. If you hold specialist skills, now is the time to tell your ideal client. Why? Because by this stage of reading your profile, they want to start seeing proof of your qualities. Including all the skills and practical experience you have, ideally, backed up by testimonies and endorsements from existing or previous clients, will spark interest and add credibility to your profile.

You'll want to show off your specialist skills and expertise in order to impress your audience, so think about those skills most relevant to your ideal client. What particular expertise are they looking for and how do your skills match to their requirements? Also, be sure the top three most relevant skills you wish to be recognised for are listed first.

Once you have done that, you'll then need to include some endorsements from respected clients. Similar to reviews, these can be influential to anyone considering your services. Take advantage of the opportunity to display them on LinkedIn. Try and keep your endorsements to a minimum rather than getting too carried away though. As always, focus on quality rather than quantity.

NICK'S TIPS

Try and get endorsements from people you already have good relationships with, particularly those who are highly skilled within your field and can vouch for the skills you want to be endorsed for. It's been known for the LinkedIn algorithm to favour more credible endorsements, so bear that in mind.

Ask for and Give Recommendations

Recommendations are critical for your profile and I strongly urge you to make the most of them, in the same way we looked at the importance of reviews in the previous chapter. **Recommendations provide great social proof of who you are and can often be the deciding factor in whether**

a prospect will reach out to you or not. The more of them you display the better. Try to gather quality recommendations from some of your key connections and remember to give them out too, this is equally as notable as receiving them.

If you can get some video testimonials from clients, even better, then include them in your summary section, as adding videos to your profile can help boost your visibility and credibility. Client endorsements can help show the world what you're made of. These are insightful for visitors as it gives them a chance to view a video of an actual client's honest thoughts and feelings. Be careful not to overdo it though, I would suggest 2-3 videos are more than enough.

Best of all? The addition of video content to your profile will really help with your ranking position from LinkedIn's algorithm. A video testimonial is among the most influential and commonly viewed pieces of media on profiles and can really prove to be a worthwhile addition.

EXERCISE 1

Make a list of the top 10 clients you think you have done some great work for and have a good relationship with. Shortlist 3 of them and ask for a video testimonial. Then reach out to the remaining and ask for a written recommendation. Now upload these to your LinkedIn profile.

Creating Consistent Content

Now that you've optimised your profile to a professional standard, it's time to start pushing out some great content. Before you start searching for anyone, you need to make sure your LinkedIn profile is attractive to prospective clients and one they might wish to respond to. If you are aiming to generate quality leads, you must show your ideal clients that you are active and valuable.

The next thing you have to do is **get used to creating regular and consistent content to publish on LinkedIn.** You will find that creating some top-quality content can prove to be a significant part of your lead generation campaign. The topics and style will depend on your target audience, your budget and your personal skill-set.

You should be adding content on LinkedIn for the same reason you should produce it for any of your other business platforms: to offer value. **People want value.** If they are encouraged to click on your LinkedIn profile, they may well be positively surprised to see you giving away free information, advice and expert opinion. It's stuff which you would normally ask for a client to pay for, so it's a nice way to immediately show them you are a valuable resource.

And by offering this extra service at no cost, you immediately show how far you are willing to go to help them. By creating good quality content, you:

- Help your LinkedIn page draw in traffic from interested sources.
- Will rank higher thanks to having more diverse, optimised content overall.
- Have another highly popular platform online in your portfolio, to promote your business and services.
- Instantly encourage any potential client to listen to what you have to say.
- Build trust by giving out content without them having to invest anything.
- Engage naturally with potential clients through likes, shares, recommendations and comments.
- Encourage other people to get in touch to see if you can also advise them with their issues.

As a professional, these things are vital to your long-term success. If you are serious about growing your client base, then you should have a plan of action in place to make it possible.

How you do this will be dependent on you and your business. My main recommendation though, would be to look at market and knowledge gaps not covered by your main competition. What are they not saying that they should be? How could you build on the content they have and make yours better? What could you do to make yourself stand out from your competition?

While it might take time to come up with a strong content marketing strategy for your LinkedIn page, once you see what gains the right response, it's easy to build it up from there.

Joining LinkedIn Groups

To help maximise the spread of your visibility, I recommend you start joining LinkedIn Groups. It's one of the best ways to begin interacting with fellow professionals who may need your help. If you are primarily using LinkedIn for lead generation, then Groups are very fertile ground. So long as you get used to working within Groups, you can find a lot of members who need your advice.

The main reason why you should pay more attention to LinkedIn Groups is because people literally join them to find help and assistance. They make excellent places to find your ideal client, or prospective clients who are very close to connecting with you. It's the perfect setting for you to add value, contribute to relevant discussions and build relationships.

It also provides you with an opportunity to start sharing some of your best articles, resources and content. You'll get more use doing that here, as the members you'll be helping out are actively using LinkedIn to find more information. Groups is where a lot of discussion around common problems, industry specific news and changes in regulations takes place on the platform, so actively contributing to group discussion is likely to get your name recognised as a valuable member. This will only be achieved though, if you are smart about the way you interact. The 80/20% rule applies here. Share 80% of interesting content, and only 20% self-promotion. By posting valuable content you position yourself as an expert in your field. The chances are curious members will then visit your profile where they will come across your website.

Keeping that in mind, you should join relevant LinkedIn Groups. To do so, all you have to do is:

1. Head to the Groups page, usually found on the top right-hand side of the LinkedIn interface.
2. Then, click on Discover. If your profile is well-optimised, the suggestions made should be credible.
3. Carry out a search using your preferred keywords, those that you've been using so far for all your marketing.
4. You are sure to find some very useful groups just with your normal keywords. Select those which are primarily aimed at the kind of clients you can legitimately target and work with.

With the potential to join as many as 100 Groups at once, it's easy to network in a mix of them that encompass your targeted client industries, markets, localities and the like. Done right, LinkedIn Groups can really help you to start engaging and impressing an almost tailor-made audience.

Social Selling Index

Before I get to the most exciting part of your LinkedIn strategy, it's probably worth mentioning a bit about a handy metric tool: Social Selling Index (SSI). If you are wondering what SSI is, it's a metric tool introduced by LinkedIn which is used to determine how well you are leveraging the platform for Social Selling, on a score between 1-100, as shown in Fig. 9.1. It helps indicate how effectively you are building a professional brand, connecting with the right audience, engaging with relevant discussions and building real relationships. This enables you to become a more refined marketer which will be advantageous to your long-term growth.

Since your aim on LinkedIn is to sell your services, you need to understand how to go about doing that accordingly. Naturally, your SSI score is only going to improve if you get used to creating your professional persona, the one which speaks to your ideal client. It's not just about having a complete and up to date profile that affects your SSI score, this will be determined by a combination of factors, so it's essential to take everything into account.

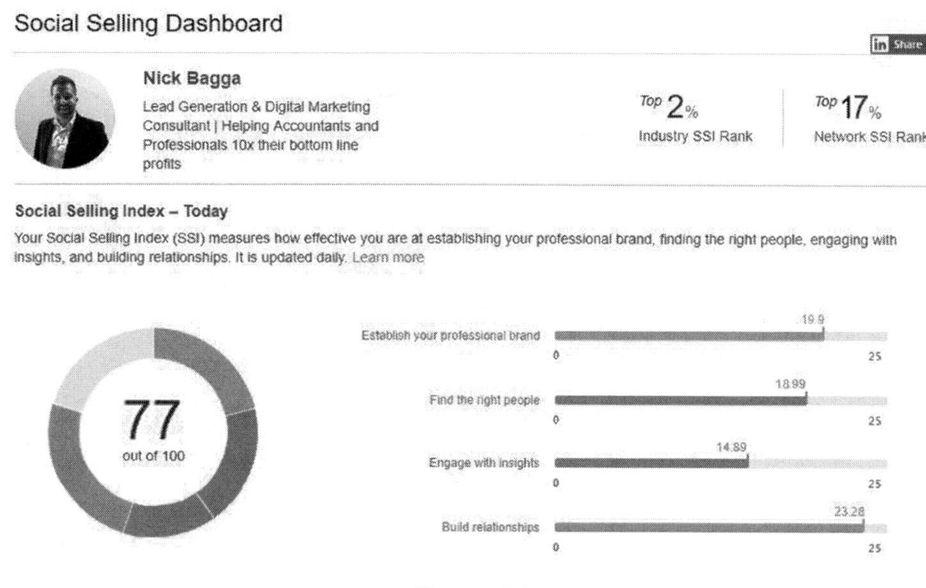

Figure 9.1

Improving Your SSI Score

You have to regularly engage on LinkedIn to improve your SSI score. I recommend you try and pay attention to the following:

- Filling out your professional profile and making sure you include meaningful content for your readers. This follows on from what I have already mentioned, but do also look through each stage of your profile and ask yourself: 'Would I hire myself if I were in their shoes?'

- I'll touch more on it in a moment, but using smart search tools like Boolean search help you to specifically locate your ideal client. This allows you to target people more effectively, improving your SSI score, as LinkedIn sees you connecting and networking with the right people.
- Your LinkedIn profile will be judged not just on the quality or regularity of content, but also the level of insight and engagement you offer. Aim to create more content which inspires discussion, debate and conversation.
- Develop content around relevant and topical industry news too. If you have quality content you are permitted to share, then do so using LinkedIn Pulse. This allows for you to build up leads quickly and regularly, generating more interaction, thus improving your SSI score.
- Make the most out of the LinkedIn Groups function. Join up to local business groups, and participate with proven tips and sound advice as often as you can. This will only help boost your SSI score as you interact with others related to your industry.
- LinkedIn offers a powerful solution for getting past the middle man and talking to decision makers instead. Use that to your advantage, making connections with more than one decision maker per target client to ensure you are more easily noticed and remembered.
- Lastly, take a look at the response rate for anyone you are going to message, checking they are active. If you contact 4 members who each have a 25% response rate, you have probably just wasted 3 messages. Try to avoid wasting connection requests and messages.

If you implement the above tips and tricks, you should see your SSI metrics showing increased scores. Your profile is then likely to rank higher as you will be ticking every box in terms of those criteria that LinkedIn looks for in its valued members.

Alright, so now that you're at a stage where you can bring in some benefits to your business, it's time to do so. Hopefully you'll now have a profile which is highly optimised, a content marketing plan in place and a high level of engagement. What now?

EXERCISE 2

Check out your own SSI score before and after you've applied the tips and tricks above. Just go to linkedin.com/sales/ssi and you should see the kind of results that you receive once you start engaging more and driving interaction amongst others, making you a valued member of the network.

Creating an Effective Lead Generation Campaign

It's time to get into the more exciting bits now, although what you've learned so far should have helped you understand what LinkedIn can offer. One of my favourite things to do is build strong relationships to generate leads and convert those leads into sales. You might be wondering why you would use LinkedIn to generate leads as opposed to any other social platform? My answer is, 'Why wouldn't you? In fact, if you're not using LinkedIn as part of your lead generation strategy, you're missing out massively. LinkedIn, for professionals, is the number one platform when it comes to lead generation. For people in your position especially, it's incredibly powerful.

With that in mind, let's see how to start using LinkedIn to develop your long-term lead generation campaigns. It's important to note that there are numerous tactics that can be employed to generate quality leads on

LinkedIn, but I'll just be explaining a basic system which gets you started, suitable for beginners or intermediate users. When it comes to generating leads, there is a four-step process which works very well. I use this for most of my clients, and I recommend you follow all four steps too. They all work together so you get the best results from the process.

So, how can you go about generating high-quality leads on LinkedIn?

Step 1: Finding Prospects

Earlier in the book, there was a conscious effort made to put together an outline of your ideal client. Well, being able to understand the kind of language and terminology a client might use is part of your appeal to them. When you carry out a search to find prospects, try to gain insight into their mindset from their choice of words. Your profile should demonstrate you are comfortable with any technical terms and jargon relating to their industry. You need to be able to speak in a way that your ideal client would understand if you wish to attract them. Doing this is much easier than you may assume.

One tool you are going to use to help you find prospects is known as the Boolean search. It's one of the oldest tricks in the book when you want a very specific answer from an online search query, and something I've used for many years. In this section, I'll show you how to make sure you get the best results from it.

Boolean search is a useful tool for both beginners and advanced users. To help you make the most of this kind of search though, it pays to know how to use it correctly. You can easily filter your search to have results which are an exact match, removing needless others which might pop up. You can ensure each search result includes or excludes certain words.

The ease of use of this function really cannot be overstated either. Thanks to the Advanced Search tool, you are able to pinpoint who you wish to target and who you wish to avoid!

With a Boolean search then, you carry out searches which are much more refined and specific to your professional needs. Let's say you are looking to target businesses within the property sector. If you were to do a simple LinkedIn search for 'property developer', you would get results which use both 'property' and 'developer', even if they are not together. This means getting a lot of extra unwanted search results coming through.

The easiest way around this is to use a Boolean search. So, in this example, all you have to do is:

- Use a search which includes "property developer" using speech marks. This way, you search results will only return those profiles with those exact same words next to each other. This will give a more targeted search result and eliminate unnecessary elements from the search parameters.
- The alternative is that you could broaden your search by using OR, so you could try looking for "property developer" OR "property investor" which would then give you results based on these related terms.
- For a more complex search, combine terms using brackets. For example, you could carry out a search for property AND (developer or investor) which is likely to produce results for property developers *and* property investors.
- Looking at this from another perspective, it's possible to remove a potential search option altogether. For example, if you only wanted to look for CEOs of large companies and not business owners, directors or consultants, use the Boolean search as follows: CEO NOT Owner NOT Director NOT Consultant as shown in Fig. 9.2 below.

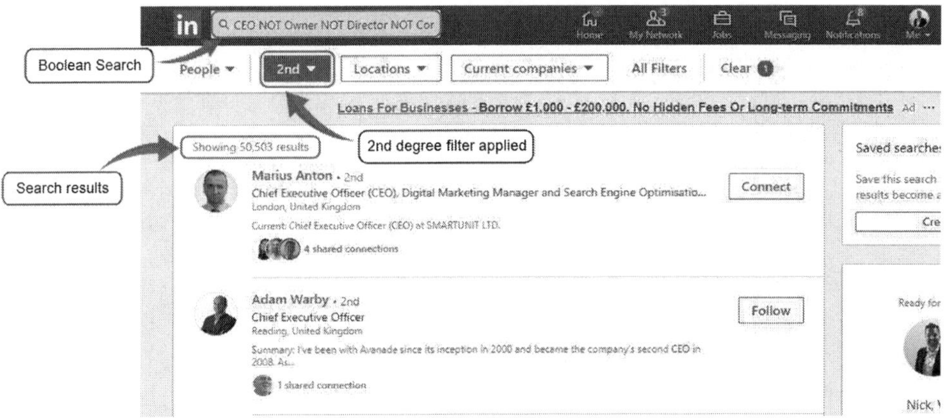

Figure 9.2

From Fig. 9.2, I have managed to narrow my search results for CEOs from circa 5 million to 50,000 using the Boolean search and filters. I could bring the number down even further using more of the filter options available such as Location, if I so wished.

As you can see, the Boolean search is a powerful tool, and will make it very easy indeed for you to hunt down more targeted prospects by narrowing your search requirements. At the very least, it will help you to remove any individuals who would not be interested in your service or would not suit your ideal client profile.

NICK'S TIPS

Be sure to use the filters available to refine your search results even further. For example, you can use the LOCATION option to specify your results geographically. Also remove 1st degree connections from your search parameters as they are already part of your network. Therefore, just use 2nd degree connections instead. This way you will achieve more specific and targeted search results.

EXERCISE 3

Practice using the Boolean search tool. Think of some examples of ideal clients you would like to find. Use the tips above to start working towards finding the right client profiles. With the help of the Boolean search, you can easily find at least 10 potential targets. If it's done right, you should be able to locate several specific profiles that could make great leads. You could start off by searching for clients you have already worked with in the past, just to get familiar with using Boolean search.

Step 2: Engaging with Those Prospects

Now that the hard part is done, it's time to learn how to introduce yourself and engage with your prospects accordingly. You should send a personal message to the individual, writing it from scratch each time. **This is crucial as making it personalised will be in direct correlation to your success rate**. The amount of times I have received unsolicited messages from individuals trying to sell me something instantly without building any kind of rapport is shocking. It's like trying to sell someone a product in the street by just shoving it in their face. If you want to make this work for you as it should, you need to be intelligent and, most importantly, respectful to the person on the other end of the message.

Just think about the number of times you receive a generic, automated message. Isn't it frustrating? Consider, does it make you feel valued in any way or likely to engage in conversation? I know these don't earn a positive response from me!

Remember you are not always going to win when it comes to relationship building. That's just life and something you should accept gracefully. I had a CFO approach me at one of my workshops once, he told me he had been looking for a marketing consultant for some time to help him with his own LinkedIn profile but couldn't trust the 'spammy type' messages he was receiving from people on LinkedIn. He said he just wanted someone genuine to build a relationship with him and earn his trust first, before any sales conversation was had. I explained to him that, sadly, most people do not understand the engagement process and expect instant gratification. We sat down and talked for an hour after the workshop. That CFO is now one of my ideal clients and we have a superb relationship. The point I'm making here, is that giving someone great value generates respect and trust which puts you in a better position to gain more business. If you adopt the same approach online, it will give you great results!

While each introductory message you send should be unique and personable, it shouldn't be too casual in tone. After all, since you are connecting with someone you do not know, it's best to avoid being too informal. The first thing they will want to know is why you are contacting them, so your message must be short, swift, and to the point. Why you are contacting them, of course, is to try and get them to move to Step 3 below.

Take a look at the prospect's profile and work out why that profile appeared in the search after using the qualifiers in Step 1. Create a message (maximum 300 characters, not words) and then make sure that in this message you include at least one of the following:

- A problem which you noticed the individual is having.
- A reference to some content they uploaded or shared, ideally asking a question they can reply to you with about the piece.
- A compliment of some form on their content, profile or business achievements.

This is a charm offensive, so be sure that you introduce yourself in a brief and positive manner. End the message with a simple request to connect with the individual on LinkedIn.

Remember to add as many contacts as you know in real-life too. People are much more likely to respond to you if they see you have other connections, particularly people in their industry or line of work.

Now you have suitably engaged with the prospect you then need to keep the conversation going. This means you shouldn't just dive straight in with the big sell: take the time to develop a relationship in order to make the prospect eventually turn into a client. That's going to require some effort, but it's an essential part of the four-step process. So, let's look at the next step.

Step 3: Developing an Authentic Relationship

Once you've had a brief dialogue with your prospect, you now need to commence building a good relationship by continuing the conversation to gain some momentum and add value. Remember, do not introduce your services or try to push for a sale. Instead focus on them and their needs, get to know them and let the conversation flow naturally.

Don't force it! Developing this relationship is a bit like dating: play it cool and drop in a compliment here and there. Don't overdo it though, or you may not hear back from your prospect. Patience here will prove to be productive for prospecting and winning.

If you have a link to a good resource you think could solve a stated problem on their page, or answers a question they have posted, then include a link and encourage them to check it out.

This shows you are listening to their needs and offer more value than your competition. Make it clear the article or content provided is merely to help them and is by no means a request for anything in return. Keep it friendly and avoid making any pitches or suggestions of a pitch, for now you are just a fellow professional making conversation and sharing knowledge.

How you structure the message is very much up to you. Include something of value, ensure its complementary in tone and the content is personal to that individual. Once you do this, you are ready to move on to the all-important fourth and final step.

Step 4: Encouraging Your Prospects to Take Action

If you have got to this stage, things are looking good. You now need to take the conversation offline, as it's offline that you convert a prospect into a client. No relationship with a prospect should be kept strictly online when you start to pitch. If you've built rapport, provided some good value and earned their trust, you should have no problem arranging a phone call or even a meeting in person. This is where you'll really get to connect with your prospect by understanding their challenges and goals and showing them how you are the solution to their problem. You may be wondering how long you should wait before taking the conversation offline. I would suggest waiting at least a week to ten days minimum before initiating any kind of offline manoeuvre.

Why this works should be obvious. You don't make it feel like you have some kind of sales funnel inspired trap to get their interest. It also makes sure they are at a point where they can understand **who you are, what you offer and why you would be useful** to them. So long as you have developed some mutual respect before you make a pitch, this should be relatively easy.

For example, you could send them a message telling them that, in the last couple of days, you worked with someone who is in their industry. Tell them a few things popped up in discussion with the other person which you'd like to share with them. Be careful to first make sure they are actually interested in the services you offer.

I personally think offering a few trade secrets or pieces of professional advice over the phone or via an email is a good move. The insights which you just offered them after working with someone else? Offer them out for free as part of a thank you for their attention.

However, the challenge here is learning how to craft quality messages which are going to give the reader something to encourage them to get back to you. Read back all your interactions with them so far, and you should see a clear pattern emerging.

Of course, they might say no and that's fine. Nothing ventured, nothing gained. They might already have an accountant, or they just might not have the budget to scale up at present. While everything you've done to refine the search should limit the chances of this, it's going to happen from time to time.

Personalising your messages and avoiding pushing too hard, though, is essential to building the rapport you need. At the very least, that individual might contact you later down the line, keeping you in mind when they are ready to scale things up.

In fact, this has happened to me on multiple occasions, where I have engaged in conversation with a prospect and then the same prospect has reached out to me several months later and become a client. Remember not everyone is 100% ready to buy there and then. The most critical part is building rapport and focusing on delivering value consistently. Don't presume that you have wasted your time if the prospect does not become a paid-up client come the end of the first week or month.

You have planted the seed. That is more than enough for now.

So, now you're at a point where you know how to use LinkedIn to a good level, let's take a look at some other social media platforms which you could be using. While LinkedIn is by far the best platform for B2B lead generation, I recommend you try and at least dip your toes in the water of those I'll go through in the next chapter.

Takeaways

- LinkedIn is easily among the most powerful social media tools for lead generation when targeting business clients, if used properly.
- Getting to grips with LinkedIn will require you to refine your profile and make sure that it's optimised for both search visibility and to attract quality leads.
- The Social Selling Index metric tool can be helpful to identify how well you are leveraging LinkedIn. You should constantly be engaging and interacting with your target audience.
- Having a content marketing strategy in place and participating in Groups will go a long way to gaining exposure, promoting your services and attracting ideal clients.
- Through smart searching parameters, you can easily avoid wasting valuable time and resources on profiles of individuals who are not key decision makers or in your target market.
- You must follow the four-step process for generating and converting leads, being patient and taking your time to ensure each lead fits your ideal client profile. When the time is right, an offer to take things offline is the perfect way to convert a lead into a client.

CHAPTER 10

GET SOCIAL: FACEBOOK, YOUTUBE, INSTAGRAM & TWITTER

Chapter 9 focused on the importance of LinkedIn to your long-term success. It's one of your most relevant social media platforms, but it's by no means the *only* viable one. In this chapter, I want to open your eyes to the power of the 'big five'; **Facebook, YouTube, Instagram, Twitter** and **LinkedIn**. Each of these play a role in your personal and professional development and lead generation activities, so it's vital you get used to working with them. It's necessary to understand how they can all help you and your business grow.

Although the others probably won't be as useful to you as LinkedIn for lead generation, which is by far the best platform for professionals, I'll discuss how they can also provide leads and sales, if leveraged effectively. The social web can be a very cost-effective way of marketing your business.

Let's get right into the nitty gritty of it all then, starting with the most diverse offering available: Facebook.

Facebook

Most people want to avoid using Facebook as they feel it's too competitive, but we're going to look beyond that. With a whopping 2.32 billion monthly active users and still growing, it's easy to see Facebook has massive potential. What's more, five new profiles are created *every single second*, meaning you may find new prospects showing up when you keep searching. It's also got over 80 million pages set up by small and medium sized businesses, so you certainly won't be alone in using it for business purposes and suggests lots of opportunities available to you.

Why you need Facebook is fairly simple: people use it all the time. It offers you so much control over who you target, and when. It puts your business in front of millions of people daily. With so much insight available on Facebook you can really drill down further to build a strong picture of your ideal clients and target them using the Facebook Ads Manager.

How you manage your Facebook account is going to be a matter of personal preference. Facebook is a massive topic, and I don't want to bog you down with over-thinking about it. To help you make the most of it, I do recommend you keep the following ideas and principles in mind.

Facebook Profile & Facebook Page: What's the Difference?

As a consultant and trainer, you'd be surprised if I told you how many people I come across who don't realise what the difference is between a Facebook Profile and Facebook Page, and which one they should use for their business. I can understand their confusion though, considering Facebook has changed terminology so frequently in the past, which certainly doesn't make it any easier to keep up with Facebook trends.

What's the difference then?

A Facebook Profile is your personal account, the one you would use to add friends and family members, communicate on a personal level and share photos, videos and general life updates. Everyone who joins Facebook gets a Profile when signing up. You can only ever have one under your name. Just think of your Facebook Profile like your main registered account. It's only after you have set up a Profile that you are ready to move on to create a 'Facebook Page' for marketing your business. Make sense? Great.

A Facebook Page then, as mentioned, is the one that would be used for your business. These are the opposite of Facebook Profiles. They are for corporate entities, brands and organisations as well as celebrities or brand influencers, as opposed to regular individuals like you and I. Pages don't have 'friends' but instead they have 'followers' or 'follows', based on the number of people who interact with and 'like' the Page. It's a seemingly small but critical distinction. A Facebook Page is what you want to create, to help market and represent your business and to develop for any kind of social media marketing.

As a professional, it's vital you keep your business promotions coming through here. This is your firm's dedicated site on Facebook, allowing visibility on this platform. To set up your Facebook Page, you will need to simply create one and make sure it stands out from the crowd. How you do that is simple – just follow the steps below.

1. To set one up, you simply need to head on over to facebook.com/pages/creation. If you don't have a Facebook account already set up, Facebook will prompt you to create one before you are able to set up a Facebook Page. Alternatively, if you already have a Profile set up then simply go to the 'Create' button on the menu bar at the top and select 'Page', as shown in Fig. 10.1.

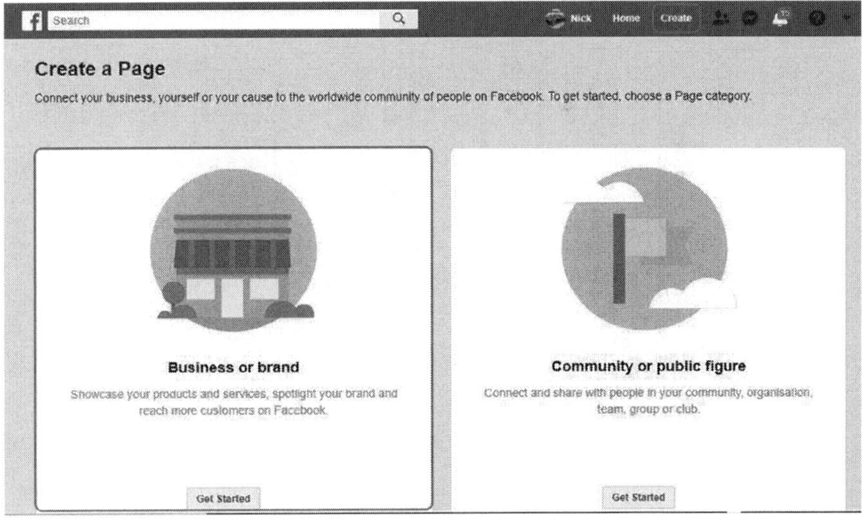

Figure 10.1

2. For your firm, I recommend choosing 'business or brand' as your Page style. Select the relevant category to represent your business in terms of what you offer. Add in your address and contact details, and then fill in the profile picture with a company logo, the same one you used for your LinkedIn cover photo should do the trick here. Make sure it fits by previewing the logo to ensure nothing is cropped out of the image. I'd also recommend adding a cover photo for completeness. This could be an image of your offices or anything you feel would be appropriate to represent your firm in a positive, friendly way. Try not to be too generic in your choice.

3. Voila! You now have a Facebook Page representing your business created in a matter of minutes. Then start building and optimising your Page by going down the left-hand side bar menu, like you did with your LinkedIn profile. Add in your 'About' section and start telling others who you are and what you do. Make this as unique as possible and remember, you want to stand out. Differentiation is the name of the game. I would keep it short and sweet. Sometimes less is more.

4. Next, add in the services which you provide. Try and highlight your most prominent professional services, particularly with one eye on getting your ideal client to take action. If you aren't sure what kind of services to list, look at the Pages of your competition. It's essential you list all the services which you intend to promote.

5. Create some posts. Try to provide new and unique content, particularly aimed at answering frequently asked questions and, perhaps, linking to some of the other resources shown on your website. This will help you to develop some critical links to your Page. Also, make sure you fill up the page to ensure it appears busy. A blank or empty-looking Page won't seem worth following, so produce some posts to gain attention and, hopefully, draw interaction.

6. Invite your friends over from your personal Profile as this will be linked automatically. This could be a great place to start to draw in some actual followers and kick start some engagement. Use the 'Invite Friends' option to encourage any social media friends you have on Facebook from your Profile to like your new Page. Also, if you have lots of your clients on email, import your email contacts list in too. Do this at the end, as your Page is not yet ready to be shared.

7. One last thing I suggest you do is to look at your username: it's normally a mixture of your business name and a random set of numbers thrown together. Change this to something which suits. I recommend your primary keyword (if possible) or a variant of those used in other marketing material.

Confirm all your details, double check everything for accuracy and completeness, then make sure you head on over to the Help page. This will give you some practical information which you could use to your advantage about further controlling, managing and improving your Page.

Facebook Groups & Events

Facebook Groups are extremely useful and can be a great way to build consensus and draw interest to your services. Groups are another way of interacting with people and offering your expertise to help those in need. It's a fantastic way to build potential partnerships too, which can grow your business exponentially.

You need to try and get involved with as many different means of drawing attention to your business on Facebook, and Facebook Groups is one of the quickest and most effective ways of doing that. The reasons why you should make sure your Facebook Page and Groups are singing from the same hymn sheet include:

- Your Facebook Page will help you to add to your online visibility as a professional and allows you to directly communicate with your target audience.
- By having access to a Group which links back to your Page, it's easy to promote your expertise within the group and add new members.
- The Group then works as a community that enables you to further display your knowledge, answering questions and providing advice.
- Within the Group you can provide extra value and tips to those drawn from your Page, showing members you care and want them to succeed.

The challenge here is learning how to use Facebook Groups in a way that benefits you. If members are going to get notifications of your updates, then these need to be more than cat GIFs and funny jokes! You should be offering posts that are relevant to the concerns of those you are targeting. This is another online space where you want to give out advice which answers some of those FAQ's. Before you set up a Facebook Group, make sure you are 100% ready to deliver top quality content to it on a regular basis.

Starting a Group is nice and simple: all you have to do is go to your personal Facebook Profile, and check for the Groups page on the left-hand side. Hit 'Create Group' and follow through the process. Simply pick a name for the Group and then start inviting some members to join it: **ensure all invitees will find relevant information waiting for them here or there is not much point in them joining!**

To begin with I'd recommend setting your Group as 'Open', so others can be invited to join, or even stumble across it by accident and request that they be added. When you get the hang of Groups, you are in a position to start setting up private groups to target more specific individuals. Also make sure you head into the Edit Settings section and ensure you tell your Facebook Profile to update you when you receive a post or comment from a member or a message via messenger.

Of course, the flipside here is that you should probably join other Facebook Groups too. This is a great way to add to your network: just like you would do with the LinkedIn Groups which I spoke about above. Simply send a request to join Groups of an adequate member size that includes people you think would be interested in what you have to offer, don't just start joining any old Group and promoting your services!

Facebook Events

Another great feature you should turn to is Facebook Events. When advertised via your Page and your Group, you can draw plenty of visitors to your Facebook Events. This allows you to promote workshops, public events, speaking sessions and various other programmes you run online or locally.

For an accounting firm, this could help you to advertise informative events you offer which cover topical content. For example, you could run workshops on Making Tax Digital (MTD) to help others better understand the tax implications of this and advise them on what steps they should take to cope with the coming changes. Events are something we'll look at a bit closer in the next chapter, but it's an important part of using Facebook to your advantage.

Why you should be hosting events is obvious: they help you to showcase your skills and draw in new prospects and leads. Anyone who comes along to one of your events is going to be very interested in what you have to say, making them fantastic individuals to connect and network with for the long-term. The more specialist and specific a workshop, the more select your attendees are going to be. No doubt a few good workshop ideas to run and promote via Facebook Events have just sprung to mind, so note them down!

Facebook Events can be set up from your Profile or Page. It's not as terrifying as it first might seem. The steps you have to follow are:

1. Head on over to your Facebook Page and go to the Events option in the left-hand side menu bar. Click the 'Create Event' button and

you'll get a new pop up screen appearing where you can edit the form for your Event.

2. You'll need to include a photo and fill in various details, such as a name for the Event and also a date. For example, you could post an event to push a month-long promotion of X% off for one of your tax services.

3. Now, fill in the section titled 'What are you planning?' and make sure it's fully informative. The first 25 characters will be displayed on invitations, so make those first few words count.

4. You'll also need to fill in an address or location: if this is a promotion rather than a normal event, then just keep this to be the address of your business.

5. Add a description of the Event or promotion in the 'More Info' section. This should be worded so that it draws interest from the right type of attendee.

6. Click on the 'Select Guests' option and start sending out invites to the interested contacts from your personal friends list.

7. I recommend you avoid inviting too many people: keep your Events tied and targeted specifically. Your closest friends might not want more business-related messages from you!

8. You can also add in a personal message which I recommend you do. Make it nice and friendly, without being too specific, as it should speak to everyone.

9. Now, give the Event a read over and ensure you are happy with it. When you feel like you have entered all the pertinent details, this is the time to act.

Facebook Ads & Facebook Retargeting

Facebook Ads and Facebook Retargeting are huge topics on their own, so I only wish to touch on them briefly here without frying your brain. These are akin to Pay-Per-Click (PPC) marketing and Google Ads, which was covered in Chapter 6. **They are targeted forms of advertising using specific parameters to pick out the individuals who will see the ads.** They can be very persuasive, but it's easy to make mistakes with them if you are not sure what you are doing.

Why should you use Facebook Ads then? To begin with it's the single strongest, most effective tool for targeting people via Facebook. No other form of paid marketing really offers the same kind of scope as the Facebook Ads Manager. You can target individuals based on location, age, income, likes and many other factors. This helps you to further promote those workshops mentioned above.

Let's say you want to run a workshop in Chiswick, West London; you could set up your Facebook ad campaign to *only* target people from Chiswick. You could also target certain types of individuals from specific professional backgrounds or businesses. If your ideal client is a business owner in the Chiswick area who earns at least £300,000 in turnover, select these parameters for your ad campaign so it only targets that audience. The power it offers is incredible, although it can sometimes be a touch overwhelming at first. In time, you'll get familiar with it and can make the most of its potential. However, the challenge in using Facebook Ads is that most people aren't on Facebook to be sold products or services; they are there to have fun, to socialise and to interact. Therefore, you can't target people based on the fact they are actively looking for what you offer.

With Google Ads, you are able to actually target people based on the fact they are searching for your services. While someone might appear on Facebook asking, 'does anyone know a good accountant in LOCATION?' or 'I need help with my accounts – anyone know someone in LOCATION?', it's not going to happen consistently. Facebook advertising then, in my opinion, is going to be a lot less suited to marketing business services compared to Google Ads or LinkedIn.

Personally, I'd recommend holding back from Facebook Ads until you've had some success with Google Ads. Instead use Facebook to generate some interest via the free solutions it includes, such as participating in Groups as well as creating your own to drive some traffic to your business.

Once you have a sizeable following and you are seeing success from other forms of paid marketing, you may wish to take this further. If you do feel brave enough to start practicing and playing around with Facebook Ads, head on over to facebook.com/business to get started.

Facebook Retargeting, also known as remarketing, follows on from your Facebook ad campaign and takes things a step further. As the name suggests, retargeting is essentially displaying your ads on Facebook to those individuals who have already checked out your website or landing page and shown some interest in what you have to offer. But then they have left for whatever reason without making a purchase or completing a Call-to-Action.

Retargeting is cookie-based technology that follows your audience around the web using a simple bit of Javascript code. This bit of code can also be referred to as a 'Facebook Pixel'. How it works is relatively simple. You place the pixel (a small bit of unobtrusive code) on your website. It's unnoticeable to your site visitors and doesn't affect your site's performance, so don't worry. It's kind of like sticking a tracking device on anyone who visits your website so that you retarget those same visitors later on Facebook in the form of Facebook Ads.

You can quite easily create your Facebook pixel (code snippet) by simply going into your Facebook Ads Manager. Once you have this, all you need to do is drop this bit of code into your website. That's it. So now, each time a new visitor arrives at your site, the code will drop a 'cookie' into their browser, meaning they'll see more and more of your ads show up when they later go on Facebook until they finally decide the universe must be telling them something!

So, you might be wondering why you would use Facebook Retargeting to flag up your business to those visitors who have already been to your site and left without making a purchase. It's simple. It gives you another chance to convert those same visitors into sales – see Fig. 10.2. Think about it, they have already shown a level of interest in your services in the first place or else they wouldn't have visited your site. But for whatever reason, they were not able to follow through the first time – a high percentage of visitors don't. Remember people are often indecisive and prefer to look around before making a decision to buy. Therefore, retargeting simply allows you to remind those same prospects you are here to help them, drawing them back over to your site via your repeated Facebook ads.

Naturally, it's easier to convince someone to come back and invest in your services if they've already shown an interest. Retargeting, for that reason, is far more effective than targeting a cold lead. Though you won't be targeting a lot of people, your engagement will be high, as those individuals will have some level of interest already. Facebook will give you a great ad rate as your ad is so incredibly targeted, meaning you have a much higher chance of conversion.

It's important to set up a Custom Audience for retargeting your visitors. Your Custom Audience is who you want to retarget on Facebook. In this case, it's the visitors who have come to your website but left without doing anything. Again, this would simply be done in your Facebook Ads Manager by heading to the 'Audience' section. This is easy enough to do just following the onscreen prompts. It's important to note that you must first have your pixel installed before setting your Custom Audience.

Retargeting is a powerful technique, but it can be quite challenging to make it work for you properly and takes some time to master and get your head around. Again, I recommend holding back from doing this until you've had a little practice with other forms of advertising campaigns which are slightly easier, such as Google Ads.

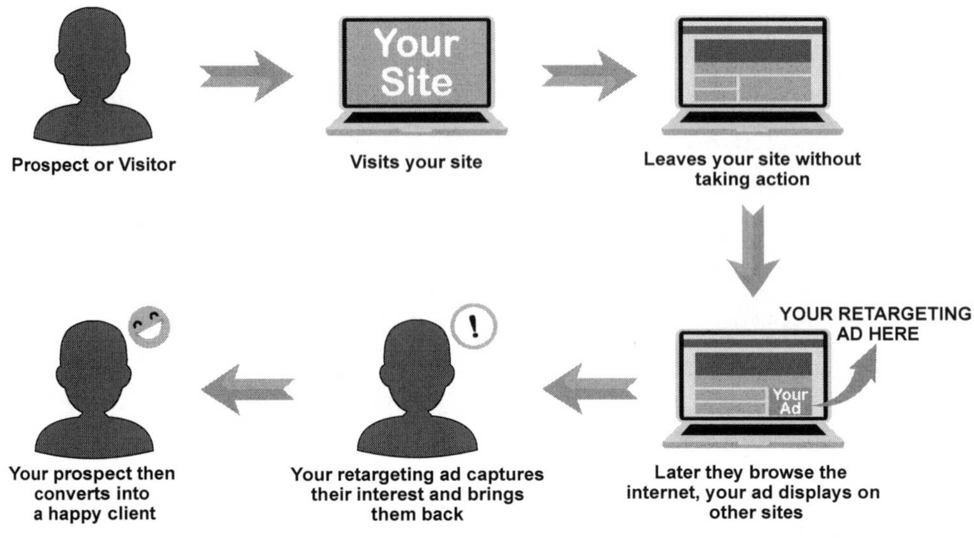

Figure 10.2

Facebook Insights

It would be unlike me not to mention a bit on Insights, considering my penchant and appreciation for numbers and monitoring results. Facebook Insights then, is another helpful feature. Not dissimilar to Google Analytics, it basically gives you a rundown of your Facebook Page's performance. It shows you some useful Page statistics which will help you make better decisions about your Facebook marketing. What good is all this marketing, after all, if you can't tell exactly how beneficial it is?

Therefore, using Facebook Insights is going to be very handy for you. It gives you various information such as:

- The total number of likes you have received.
- The number of followers your Page has and how many are interacting with your content. This could be commenting, liking, sharing or engaging in any other way.
- The total reach of your content for the last week or month, although you can't delve deeply into this as there is no option for a custom range to be set at present.

- Unique views for any post or content that you push or promote.
- The volume of users who interact with your content, compared to those who viewed it but didn't take any action.

By using Insights, you're able to determine exactly what to look out for moving forward. It helps you to see where performance is strong and where it might need to improve. This can help you to better design your content strategy going forward, as well as avoid repeating the same mistakes.

Another benefit of Facebook Insights is that it enables you to get more out of the already powerful Ads Manager. Not only will Facebook Ads become more intelligent in their targeting when using Insights, it'll boost engagement, which will, in the long run, deliver a notable increase to your ROI. Since targeting your ideal client with Facebook Ads can be somewhat challenging, Insights delivers some key information to solve that issue.

It can also help you to find out about relevant new topics which you could market, advertise and even just write about. It guides you to improving the accuracy of each campaign, ensuring you are much more likely to see your Facebook Ad campaigns target the right people and deliver the correct message. You'll soon have a mountain of new relatable topics to consider: each of them helping you to engage and interest your audience in the correct manner.

Also, be sure to adjust your Insights in order to search potential clients on Facebook, both those who use your Page as well as specific audiences built on your ideal client demographic information. From getting involved in trending topics, to offering useful advice based on frequent problems that arise in your demographic, Insights makes it much easier to know **who** and **how** to target your ideal client.

Just remember to keep reading this section on a regular basis. **How and what you do with that information will be unique to your own business and ambitions, but you should click into the Insights section at least once a week.** It's good practice to see how things are going so you are ready to make the necessary improvements going forward.

YouTube

Next on the list of useful and practical social media tools and amongst my personal favourites is YouTube. It's extremely powerful, particularly if you learn how to use it correctly and properly harness its appeal. If you think YouTube isn't a relevant tool for you as a professional, think again. With over 5 billion views every single day, it's the second most visited site on the planet at the time of writing. Add in the fact that video marketing is now used by around 81% of businesses, it's easy to see why people keep opting for it! There are billions of hours of video watched on any given day, more than enough marketing potential to tap into.

YouTube is, of course, a massively recognised social media channel dedicated to video content. It's used for everything from users posting wild conspiracy theories to covering songs of their favourite artists. For you, though, it's important to consider YouTube as it's a **fantastic, high-authority website which allows you to showcase your own credentials.**

Why, as a professional service firm, would you want to promote your services on YouTube? Simple: most of your competition will probably be having the same doubts you do about it. That means it's often an untapped source of traffic, lead generation and trust building. You could be using YouTube to post anything from top tip videos on how to save tax to a guide to setting up a new business. **You can use this platform to offer evidence of just how good you are at what you do.** The list of possibilities is endless, but you should definitely look to include videos which cover various aspects of your services.

For example, use the platform to run short webinars on accountancy best practices for business owners or position yourself as the expert for those in your ideal niche/industry to target. This could bring in a lot of attention, display your familiarity with various topics and make it easier for your viewers to trust and believe in what you have to say.

Nonetheless, creating a quality YouTube channel takes time and effort. Therefore, you need to create diverse, informative and factual content on a regular basis. You may want to create a video that recommends other quality content from respected sources from across YouTube on top of your own information, advice and education in accountancy; there are lots of options here.

However, in this section, I don't want to tell you how to go about shooting video content. This is something you should work out in-house. I do recommend one thing though, that if you feel like you aren't a capable 'actor' for the video, consider bringing someone in to do it for you. The quality of your video must be spot on, which means putting in the effort to keep it nice, smooth and professional. Getting this right will naturally take time.

As YouTube is owned by Google, having good quality YouTube content linked to your website is only going to help with your Google search engine ranking. Although the main reason why you should be looking to make your YouTube account a major part of your social media marketing toolkit, is that here you encourage people to take note of what you have to say simply by offering great value.

Let's say you are on the shortlist for selection alongside your main competitor. Your ideal client checks you and your competitor out. They see that although your reputation, rates and skills are much the same, you offer video guides which provide them with top tips on reducing expenditure, understanding their books and managing cash flow. Just like with providing a free ebook, as mentioned earlier on, it indicates you aren't aiming to monetise every simple bit of advice you give clients. Who do you think your ideal client is more likely to try out?

How to Create a Quality YouTube Channel

You now need to get to grips with the fundamentals of creating a quality YouTube channel which stands out for all the right reasons. Due to the nature of the content you will be covering, it's recommended that you keep videos about 1-3 minutes long. This is long enough for your audience to learn something beneficial and short enough to avoid them forgetting what they learned.

Creating a YouTube channel is very easy: so long as you have a Google account, you can set up a YouTube channel.

1. Start off by going to your Google account, and then checking the Brand Accounts section. In here, you create a 'brand account' which allows you to manage your entire business practice instead of posting videos under your personal name.

2. To do that, you simply need to sign in to YouTube and head over to your Channel List (normally found on the left-hand side). Once you are in here, click on 'Create A New Channel'.

3. Once that is done pick the Brand Account option from the list, meaning all content will now fall under the name of the brand, not you personally. This is essential for your business.

Note: Google, like all online services, changes how its users can create accounts from time to time. This may change in the near future.

When your brand channel is set up you will be ready to start pushing further into the creation of videos. Start by brainstorming ideas as often as possible, creating new content on a weekly basis. One video per week should be manageable for you in the short-term.

How you create and manage your videos is something you, personally, will need to think about. Aim to supply videos which answer all your frequently asked questions, as this helps you to quickly provide easy to view and absorb content and generates trust with a potential client.

Also, try and make sure you don't just re-invent the wheel. If you were going to cover a topic but notice a few of your competitors have already done this, then make that video a lower priority on your list. Think outside the box for gathering ideas and consider answers to all the potential questions your ideal client would pose to you.

If you take the time to better understand all of this, you are much more likely to produce effective long-term results. While using YouTube can be exceptionally tough, the management of your account and the uploading of content is relatively simple. So long as your videos are relevant to your audience, make use of keywords naturally in their description and are all linked to your website and your brand page, you benefit from using this more visual form of social media.

You should be prepared to work at this for the long-term. Building a viable presence on YouTube will take time, but if you avoid repeating the same content as your competition and ensure your video speaks to your ideal client, you are much more likely to gain fruitful results from using it.

NICK'S TIPS

Video marketing is so influential today and you can't afford not to consider this as part of your inbound marketing strategy to stay ahead of your competition. If you feel like you're not a camera person, why not consider using your staff to run some weekly videos. You could alternate this amongst staff members, highlighting the range of your firm's knowledge and skill sets.

EXERCISE

Jot down 5-10 ideas of the kind of videos your firm could create and upload on YouTube. Think of your target audience and your ideal clients. Have a browse on YouTube – see what your competitors are doing. Could you create something better?

Making the most of Video Testimonials on YouTube

Throughout this book, I've made the point that getting your clients to endorse you is essential. It's the lifeblood of any good business. If you want to start building up your reputation quickly, one thing to do is utilise the power of video testimonials. Given the massive visibility and scale of YouTube this makes perfect sense. It gives you the ideal way to build high-traffic video endorsements for the work you do.

I've been asked numerous times by clients of mine in the past about the power of video testimonials. I tell each and every one of them the same thing: this is an absolute must. If you want to build credibility and also bring in more views, clicks, hits and clients, you should consider using YouTube for your video testimonials. Of course, there are other platforms for these too but since YouTube is owned by Google and it's free, why would you not consider using it? Now you've learnt a bit about it and know how to create a quality YouTube channel, it does make sense to start here.

Many professional service firms rely on referrals but are reluctant to ask for testimonials, written or verbal. This astounds me every time, especially when I speak to clients and hear about the great work they are doing for their clients. I don't know whether it's a pride or status thing which makes them reluctant to ask clients for testimonials, but it needs to change! A written referral can sound good, bringing more business to you, but video recommendations will only help expedite that process by convincing new prospects, based on the evidence of your satisfied clients. You make it much easier to capture both potential clients the videos recommend your services to and draw in others looking for the kind of expertise you provide.

Endorsements are influential, making your business stand out from the competition. Nowadays, you're expected to provide new and unique ways of reaching the hearts of potential clients to convince them you are the perfect choice and solution to their needs. Video testimonials are the best way to achieve this. The sceptical nature of the internet means some people might not be 100% convinced by a written one. More importantly, text testimonials can easily be missed as part of the browsing process. They can also sound quite generic. Videos take things to the next level and make it much easier to be spotted and viewed. The audience will see a live person talking directly to them about what you have done for others. That's far more trustworthy and effective.

Benefits of Video Testimonials

I've already stressed the importance of building your authority and credibility, which video absolutely does, but now you should consider some other **key benefits** using video testimonials can give your business.

Video testimonials increase trust and incentive. Although between 80-90% of consumers trust online reviews as much as personal recommendations, many still question the authenticity of written reviews. As mentioned, they can often sound generic and quite easily be manufactured by close friends and family. Videos eradicate that doubt and increase the validity of endorsements. When clients are kind enough to record a video testimonial for you, they are putting their reputation on the line. Knowing the video will be shared in the public domain, no client will be keen to put their name on a business which doesn't live up to what they say. Therefore, potential new clients of yours are much more likely to develop trust and engage with you after watching real people say real things.

Videos generate a higher retention rate than text. There are many studies that have proven the retention rate from watching a video is significantly higher than for textual information. One of the main reasons for this is because of the emotion which videos can trigger in people. As visual beings, we are used to associating words with images. Our brains are particularly attuned to stories – and that's precisely what video testimonials provide. They can resonate and hit certain parts of our brains which make them more memorable and believable.

Video testimonials drive sales and generate new leads. The opinions of unbiased people carry more credibility as opposed to your own words of self-promotion. Though your own words will be appreciated by your audience, they will not have the same impact as video testimonials from your clients. This is one of the reasons why potential new clients get enthused by them and prompt the decision to choose a particular business. According to Aberdeen Group, video marketers get 66% more qualified leads per year and achieve a 54% increase in brand awareness.

Several of my clients have increased their own sales conversions by as much as 35% with the implementation of video testimonials. Client testimonial videos are the closest thing to in person 'word of mouth' referrals available online and a free marketing tool you can't afford to ignore to boost your sales and generate new leads.

People prefer video. There is no denying the fact that people love watching all kinds of video, including myself. Consumers prefer watching video over text. Period. Cisco has projected that more than 80% of all internet traffic will be video by 2021. The simple fact is videos are incredibly engaging and much easier to digest and interpret due to many psychological factors. It's not just consumers either though, according to a WordStream statistic, 59% of executives would rather watch a video than read text on the same topic. It doesn't matter what type of video it is, using this format will attract a much higher level of engagement from your prospects every time.

Videos can be shared for SEO benefits. The great thing about videos is that they get shared a lot more than textual or graphical information. The more social traction you get from videos being seen, liked and shared the greater the SEO benefits you will receive, in the form of backlinks and social engagement. Include your client video testimonials on your website as well as social media platforms for increased exposure. As long as you ensure they are optimised correctly, there is no reason why these cannot boost and improve your long-term SEO results.

Video Testimonial Best Practices

As you can see, using video testimonials on YouTube to your advantage is very much worth the time. Now let me share some **best practices** for making the most of your client video testimonials.

Get Your Video Testimonials to Focus on the 'Why'

This is the ultimate best practice for creating video testimonials. It's to show **why** you are the best choice for a potential client. This not only helps to build a valid emotional connection with the viewer, but it also tells them you can assist with their pain points.

These testimonials should be more than an endorsement of your capabilities and competencies. While they should highlight your key skills, it's better to focus on what you have done for your client and why it has made an impact on their business. Put simply, those viewing your sites, and by extension watching your video testimonials, aren't looking to learn about your features as a business. They want to know what problems you have solved, and how you solved them.

I have seen quite a few video testimonials which come across as quite generic, almost as if the person is reading from a pre-written script. They don't focus on the 'why' and fail to tell a story. If you have helped save a client a significant amount of tax or helped them expand internationally ask your client to talk about this and the contribution you have made to their success. This way, the endorsement will draw a positive response from your ideal clients making them recognise your potential impact on their business success too.

So, in your testimonials, encourage your endorser to focus on the 'why' side of things. Why did they hire you? Why did they need your help? Why were you the right advisor who met these needs? Why should the viewer take action and engage you?

Getting Social Media Traction from Video Testimonials

Another good reason to use video testimonials is because of their social media shareability. People love to be mentioned on social media especially when thanked or praised in some way, shape or form. Therefore, you could tag (reference) your clients on social media platforms like LinkedIn, Facebook and Twitter by thanking them directly. Try being a bit more strategic and praise them for their business achievements or something you feel is relevant, perhaps even in relation to something mentioned in the video testimonial itself. This way they are more likely to want to share the video so it can be viewed by their friends, contacts, followers etc.

Make sure you get these on LinkedIn as mentioned in Chapter 9. As the most likely place to find quality clients, it pays to have a good standard of testimonials on LinkedIn. It's excellent social proof and the traction you are likely to get from the shares and views will no doubt increase awareness and draw in new prospects.

Optimising Your Video Content

You should continually be editing video headings, tag lines and description data for SEO purposes. I recommend you do this as soon as possible, and if you have any previous video testimonials already posted, that you edit and update those too. Get some of your most important keywords which your ideal clients are searching for included in the main headline, the main description and in the search tags.

This is all easily done whether it's through your own website or for social media channels like Facebook, LinkedIn and YouTube. When uploading the file, be sure to make the descriptions and headings enticing. Try and ask a question perhaps: something to encourage both positive SEO visibility and to make it more likely that people will click on the link in the first place.

Keep your Videos Short and Sweet

I do have a quick word of caution about using video testimonials – and it's one thing to bear in mind. While video is easily accessible and more readily viewable for many, length still counts. Try and keep your video testimonies to, at most, 2-3 minutes. Sure, you may want the story and gushing praise to continue a little longer, but you equally want viewers to pay attention to the core message.

In that short couple of minutes, the video should make the case for why you proved to be helpful to a previous client, and how you are just as valuable to a potential client. Go through each testimony and try to minimise the time as much as you can without losing the strength of the message. I have witnessed clients experience the best levels of conversion by keeping a video to around two minutes.

NICK'S TIPS

When deciding on what clients of yours to get testimonies from, refer back to your ideal client profile. Think of the clients you want to attract and maybe use some existing clients that fit this to be ones you ask.

The biggest tip I can give you is *not* to use a rigid script. Give them a brief instead, detailing what you're looking for, the direction you want the video to go in, how long you want it to be and where it will be posted. This way the video will come across a lot nicer and feel natural, instead of rehearsed.

Instagram

Instagram is perhaps less effective amongst the social media platforms to promote the activities of some professional advisory firms but is great for generating leads for different types such as architects and property firms. Instagram, or IG, is an image-heavy social media platform, most commonly suited to people in athletic pursuits, fashion industries, lifestyle and photography. With millions of users already, Instagram is growing all the time and it would be foolish to ignore the rich potential it holds.

A client of mine, a firm of architects that specialise in bespoke furniture for the hospitality industry, secure 35% of their business from Instagram. My team manage the campaign and we've seen great results from posting before and after photos with minimal text.

In fact, for one of the major projects my client was working on delivering, we only posted a handful of before, during and after pics with just a few words of text and relevant, popular hashtags. That specific post generated a lead from a new chain of hotels launching in the Netherlands.

My client managed to secure the business which has brought in a tremendous amount of new revenue. This example shows just how powerful social media can be when used effectively. As you can imagine, my client was elated with the results and it all came from being able to use Instagram in an intelligent way. For some businesses, it's easy to see that Instagram could have a huge amount of potential when used to target ideal clients where images can tell a story of what they do.

Another client of mine, a real estate firm in Central London, have also managed to land two major projects from implementing very similar strategies. We posted a video of a walk-in tour of a property they worked on and added some others which showcased the progress of the property development. These simple videos were short and to the point. The firm immediately gained a lot of positive feedback and received umpteen replies and declarations of interest which they didn't anticipate initially.

A video doesn't have to be long; it should tell a quick story while encouraging the user to stick around. So long as they showcase a solution to a problem, in this case clients wanting to know what the house looked like from inside, Instagram videos and photos can be very powerful indeed.

Why you should consider using Instagram is straightforward: **Instagram is yet another way to show the human side of your business.** While you want to always come across as being professional, social media is also a great way to show you are personable and amiable. It's useful for tapping into aspects such as showing who works for you, where you work and what you do. Alongside YouTube videos, it's a great tool for demonstrating how your business is backed by passionate and informed individuals.

Instagram is a great place to put a face to a name, in a way that no other social media platform allows. For an accounting firm, photos of you having discussions with clients, meeting partners, attending trade shows and conferences, all demonstrate that your business has a dedicated and hardworking team behind the scenes.

People like to know who they are working with; it fosters a closer connection between you and your potential clients. From your pictures they are encouraged to believe you will empathise with their problems, listen to what they have to say and understand where they are coming from.

So, how can you make the most of this tool? What does Instagram offer the average accountant?

How to Make the Best Use of Instagram

While it might not be too easy to do, some of the best recommendations for using Instagram as an accountant would include:

- Showcasing a new service or feature coming into play. For example, imagine you just installed a new MTD for VAT compliance software system. A quick screenshot of the software in action is a good teaser of a new and important service you are promoting. It's going to allow the message to be seen and felt accordingly.
- Since Instagram is relatively low on interaction, it tends to be quite easy to control and manage. This enables you to post things like messages of congratulations to a client or thanking someone for their business, without getting too many interactions with it. That might not sound like a good thing, but the purpose of this kind of message is to hit the right notes with the client.
- Deliver enthusiastic messages and upbeat information. For example, a lot of your competition might be producing negative, panic-driven messages about tax deadlines. Instead of following the same tone, create an upbeat message which encourages the potential client to take action out of positivity, not fear.
- Follow individuals on Instagram and wait for the right moment to step in and introduce yourself as a solution to their problem. Yes, this will mean sometimes following accounts that are essentially a waste of your time in terms of the leads they generate. However, it could help you to grab a new client simply by pitching yourself at the right time.

- While this might not be entirely beneficial to you as a business in the accountancy practice, before and after shots can work very well. Even simple things like 'Before you save X% on expenses' and 'After you save X% on expenses' with a visibly sad, then happy, person being shown. These kinds of images resonate well and can often produce good hits and clicks to your business.

Getting the most out of Instagram for your accountancy or other professional services firm can be tough. However, the above recommendations should make it easier to start you off and then make some progressive changes.

Twitter

Lastly, that brings us on to Twitter. While Twitter is not always going to be suitable for you, it's important to understand how you could potentially use it. Unlike the other social media platforms mentioned above, Twitter is all about being short and snappy. It has a 280-character limit on a tweet, meaning you need to avoid elaborate descriptions. With Twitter, it's all about fitting quality content into a clearly defined structure, making it totally different to other social media conventions. It's like running your own personal newsletter which you update with your thoughts, theories and queries. Someone can choose to follow your account, meaning they are updated on your content via their own news feed, and they can see, share and interact with anything you post.

However, the major difference with Twitter and say, LinkedIn, is that here your content can be shared by anyone, even people you have never heard of before. Twitter is most commonly used for posting things like links to more in-depth content, promoting a product or new service and interacting with those looking for short and simple answers from you. **In other words, you should use Twitter as it allows you to easily send out short pieces of information which can be easily digested, conveyed and acted upon. Every message is like a Call-to-Action in itself.**

How to use Twitter to Your Advantage as a Professional

Again, I don't want to get bogged down in telling you how to tweet. Instead, I want to help you learn how to use Twitter to benefit from it. Firstly, head on over to twitter.com and create a profile. The process is similar to setting up any other online profile: you need to enter a name (use your business name, not your personal name), a password and an email address.

Be sure that your Twitter handle, or your username, is based on your company. For example, Joe Bloggs Accountancy firm might go for something like @joebloggsaccts, or perhaps @jbloggsaccountancy. Choose whatever you feel works best for you.

You'll now need to go through the same process as you did for your Facebook Page, optimising your Twitter profile. Thankfully, this takes a lot less time. All you have to find is an image and cover logo, your LinkedIn selections from Chapter 9 should suffice, and add a quick snappy profile about your business. Again, it's limited by word count, so include your profession, your location and a contact number. Also give out your website address here to gain another useful backlink to your site.

At this stage, then, you have to get used to tweeting properly. Here are some best practice tips to help you use your account to benefit your business:

- Make sure you take advantage of the 'Who to Follow' section. This will give you suggestions as to who you could follow based on your current followers and interests.

- You can also import your contacts from Gmail, Microsoft Outlook, Yahoo etc. Simply click on the 'Connect other address books', and 'Find people you know' section and follow the steps.

- Be sure to update all your other social media and communications channels to let them know about the new Twitter feed and request that contacts follow you there.

- Outside of just posting links to your own content and media, try and find quality content on Twitter to retweet and share with others. Offer more value-driven information compared to sales pitch content on Twitter: sales heavy tweets have a unique power to put people off.

- Try and find a nice mixture of verified local and industry news. For example, the UK Government is often changing tax policy, so you could look to provide relevant links to official content about these changes, giving your readership information they can actively learn from.

- To find good quality sources of news for your local area and your industry, type in the names of both your location and your industry, perhaps using the Boolean search I mentioned earlier. This would enable you to find appropriate Twitter accounts to follow.

- Be sure you focus on quality over quantity: just retweeting every piece of vaguely pertinent news is not going to do you much good. Look at each tweet carefully before you send it: Does it really offer value to your potential readership?

Outside of providing added value and quick links to relevant content, you can find more clients on this social media platform too. If you want to use Twitter to help find and source new clients, you need to use the right search parameters and tools.

Start off by going to the search bar and enter the name of your town. From this you receive a feed displaying lots of tweets, some of which are relevant, some less so. Start following any local businesses that appear which fall into the niche you tend to target. Look through their followers too, and you'll most likely find they'll be quite happy to follow you back.

Underneath the search query, you'll spot a bar or tab advertising the Advanced Search tool. I recommend only filling in the Location tab, sometimes known as 'Places' on certain Twitter updates. Depending on where you live, set a radius which you are comfortable with and hit search. Since Twitter content is more likely to be read from a smartphone, and people have the location switched on for these, Twitter knows where a large proportion of tweets are coming from. Start looking through profiles and before long you should be able to build up a decent number of followers.

Not everyone will follow you back but even if 30% or so choose to, then you are doing well. Trim your own followings over time, as you will likely be following individuals with no relevance to your business and little interest in what you have to say.

Lastly, the best way to use Twitter is for getting in touch with potential clients. I recommend you use it for things like:

- Sending a thank you message once they start following you.
- Interacting with users if they are asking for help on Twitter, offering expertise and advice.
- Introducing yourself to anyone who is tweeting locally about needing your services.
- Offering followers and other interested people links to helpful and supporting documents wherever possible.
- Asking questions and raising important issues with official accounts and government bodies.
- Finding out information from fellow professionals that you could use to assist a client.

Twitter can be a headache to use at the best of times, but you can get to grips with it quickly when you put in some effort. If your clientele seem to be on Twitter frequently it might be worth you using it on a more regular basis.

So, now you're at a stage where you understand and appreciate the 'big five' social media tools, let's look at some other key strategies you could use to help take your business to the next level. Some, or all, of these might not be suitable to your business but they are worthwhile considering.

Takeaways

- Using social media effectively can be hard to grasp, but the rewards from getting it right mean they are very much worth investing time and effort into.
- Through Facebook you can create a huge amount of interest and professional growth for your business within a fraction of the normal time taken by other advertising routes.
- YouTube allows for high-quality information delivery and search engine optimisation across a very popular platform on the internet. It's one of the most powerful tools available to gain exposure and increase credibility.
- Instagram has a limited purpose within professional services but can be particularly favourable to certain professional groups such as architects, real estate developers and general property firms.
- Twitter can be hard to use but it could be a resourceful tool once you get familiar with working it. Here you should be more topical and less sales driven, without trying to cover too much all in one go.
- You don't have to use every social media platform for your business – it's important to find the ones which work best for your firm and industry. Quality over quantity is always the right approach if you want to use social media to your advantage.

CHAPTER 11

EMAIL MARKETING, WEBINARS, PODCASTS & EVENTS

The last two chapters focused on good ways to advertise and grow your business via social media. There's no denying that managing social media can be challenging, but each platform can be of immense benefit to your business handled in the right way. It's now time to look at some other ways of generating quality leads through some equally impactful strategies and techniques. Social media is all well and good but let's not forget about the sheer power of **email marketing.**

Email marketing is still one of the best ways to grow your business and trumps social media platforms in terms of numbers and impact. Almost everybody uses email on a daily basis, but not all of us use LinkedIn or other social platforms nearly as much. Some treat email as if it's become outdated. But do you know anyone who *doesn't have* an email address? Enough said.

We'll also look at other marketing methods to help grow and promote your business, which include: **Podcasts, Webinars and Events**. This is all about helping you to pitch yourself as a proven expert in your field, and ensure you build and develop lasting credibility. By positioning yourself as being ahead of the professional curve, you will soon inspire others to see you as the 'go to' person for good advice.

So, without any further delay, let's get into it.

Email Marketing

If you listened to certain individuals and didn't know better, it would be easy to assume that email is an old-hat form of marketing. Some people talk about it as if it's the Latin of online marketing: dead. With the rise of things like social media it has become easy to criticise earlier online marketing methods such as email. However, the concern around email marketing is in the perception of it. People presume it's impossible to get spotted when email inboxes are loaded with everything from promotional pushes to conversations with friends.

What if I told you that email marketing has a greater impact than social media for client conversion? It's still one of the most cost-effective marketing methods which can generate a significant ROI.

At present, there are at least 3.5 billion email users in the world, according to a recent study by Radicati. These numbers are continually growing and it's almost impossible to find someone who doesn't have an email address, purely on the basis that it's been around for the best part of 50 years. Email first started in 1972 and has since become a staple of modern life. Today over half the entire planet's population uses email. **If you believe that email marketing is dying out, then you are looking at it all wrong.**

So, is email marketing still as effective as it once was? No, it's even *more* effective.

Every business you are likely to work with will have at least one company email address. Your ideal client will most likely be email fluent and happy to pay attention to multiple email accounts across the day. With billions of people to target, it should be easy to see just what kind of potential reach email marketing has in its path.

Why Email Marketing is Still King

The first thing to recognise then, is why email marketing is still such a powerful tool for you and your business. Typically, the reasons include:

- An email list is still comfortably one of the most consistent and loyal marketing methods to use.
- On average, for every £1 that you spend on email marketing, you can see as much as £44 back in ROI.
- No other form of marketing allows you to be quite so personal, or personable, as email does. You are able to be much more specific in an email message when compared to social media.
- While users might check in on their Facebook and Twitter from time to time, email is something which most people tend to check daily.
- It can easily be combined into your social media and other marketing campaigns, helping them to feed off one another for maximum impact and positive results.
- You are more likely to get spotted and noticed via email than social media, as you are less likely to get drowned out by other content, messages and topics.
- The simplicity of setting up an automated email campaign makes it possible to establish a profit-generating one with just a few easy clicks.

As you can see, everything can be amplified when using email marketing to your advantage. It's very much still sitting atop the throne of online marketing techniques. Email marketing is absolutely worth your time; as the potential benefits of it will add a punch to your marketing toolkit.

How Can You Use Email Marketing for Maximum Impact?

There are several email marketing platforms out there to get started with your email campaigns such as aWeber, GetResponse or MailChimp. These are arguably the biggest, easiest to use and most affordable tools for this purpose, where you can create email lists, contact forms, design email templates and set up pre-defined automatic email responses, to help drive your email marketing campaign forward.

Each one has their own strengths and weaknesses, but I would recommend you look at all three to determine which one is best for you. Once you sign up with any of them, filling in details about your business including the website address, you'll land on the dashboard where you then go about creating an email campaign. Most of the sites above come with a fantastic introductory system guide, so I advise you to follow that as it will help you to build your first ever email marketing campaign.

If you have a limited budget, then go for MailChimp: it allows you to mail up to 2000 recipients without having to pay anything. It's the best way to get your email marketing up and running without having to fund it upfront.

Regardless of which software tool you choose, it will provide you with all the utilities needed to implement an email campaign that can be customised and tailored to suit your audience. You'll be able to send each subscriber the appropriate message based on where they are in the sales funnel. The joy of email marketing is that you could easily split up your email contacts list to determine who should be sent a message, and at what stage. Someone who has just joined up, for example, should not be receiving the same email as someone who joined six weeks ago.

Let's move on to getting you started with MailChimp to create effective email marketing campaigns. There are 5 main steps involved in the process.

Creating an Email Marketing Campaign Using MailChimp

1. Establish your key goals

It's important you first take time to define your business goals, as discussed in Chapter 3, before going full speed ahead creating any sort of marketing campaign. Like anything else you may be doing to market your firm, it must be based on clear ground rules. Start off by establishing your key goals for the marketing campaign and relate them to your ideal client profile. I recommend you spend some time looking at the kind of questions your targets may have.

You need to ensure your marketing goals correctly align with your email marketing plan. Are you looking to bring in more clients, if so what type of clients? Or are you looking to drive sign ups to a service which you are offering? You may be aiming to upsell some of your other services to existing clients. Whatever the goal is, your campaign should reflect your primary aim(s).

However, remember that your email campaigns shouldn't be rigid. They should be aimed at your primary and ideal client but contain enough variety to attract other potential clients as well. What you could do if you're unsure and looking for inspiration is sign up to some professional services mailing lists yourself. You don't have to look at your direct competition, but those in similar (but not identical) industries could give you some good ideas on how to best plan your long-term campaign. Study these for things like, tone, message, structure, length and content to see what makes them enticing to a reader, or not. You should never start with a blank canvas, use some examples and take the time to do some research until you're clear about your goals and objectives.

2. Start building your email list

Use the subscriber details from your website's Call-to-Action to build and grow a high-quality email contact list which matches up with your primary goals established above. The primary audience you want to target, of course, are your ideal clients. Those prospects you already have and fit your ideal client profile; import their details into your email platform.

You can do this using MailChimp's import feature, from an Excel CSV file, transfer your contact list from your business email account into Excel. Simply use the Export feature which comes with your normal email package, and then upload this to MailChimp using the Import feature. However, **be sure to get in touch with every person and confirm their permission to include them in the new email list.**

You may need to consider building a new list from scratch, if you don't already have many leads or clients to include. That's not a big issue, though, as it's what you'll likely need to do for most of your marketing needs. To develop your list, you should set up a campaign for new subscribers to get this going. I'll touch on that in a moment.

For now, think about what kind of enticing offers you could use to develop your email list. From an introductory discount available on subscription to giving out unique content normally worth paying for, what would encourage people to want to sign up? When you are ready, simply head to the Campaigns page and go to Create Campaign. Then, choose Email.

Using the Campaign Builder, it's possible to build just about any kind of email campaign you wish. You'll need to include a place on your website for visitors to sign up to your email campaigns too, so those people you don't intentionally target can also join. Most of the time, the best places for this would include in a 'lightbox' (a pop up which dims the rest of your website to place specific emphasis on your website) or at the end of any posts you publish.

If someone reads to the end, they might just be convinced enough to sign up!

3. Select your campaign type

Of course, deciding the kind of campaign you want to run is going to be essential to your success with email marketing. Therefore, think about which campaign type is appropriate for each segment of your Mailchimp list. It all depends on the kinds of goals you thought about when determining Step 1, so keep those in mind as you move forward here.

MailChimp also offers some practical insight when starting any campaign, as you will notice. However, regardless of what you choose within MailChimp, there are general archetypes of mailing campaigns which you may wish to run.

Some of the most common options include, but are not limited to:

- **Newsletters.** Great for providing weekly content and updates on information about your industry, and especially to give out insights based on topical events. It helps you to issue advice, build authority and improve trust with your reader. Very useful, and every professional services firm should look to have a newsletter at one stage.
- **Announcements.** Some clients will want to sign up to this for practical advice and announcement campaigns will be relevant to send emails about your latest service changes. This could be anything from Making Tax Digital specific offers for accountants, to changes to the legal system for a lawyer. Anything you think might impact on your clients you should look to announce in this way.
- **Offers.** If you have a list of clients who are always looking for more value from what you offer, you could run an offers-specific mailing campaign. Offering introductory prices on new services you provide and telling subscribers about the latest services that might help them. Good to tie in with your newsletter and topical news in your industry.
- **Events.** Another good mailing campaign to run might be for those you wish to network and mingle with on a more regular basis. This would increase and improve the number of people attending your events, and boost awareness of important industry changes which could help them to improve their business. A good mailing campaign to run for professionals.

Of course, you should try to better understand what is going to suit your clients as time goes on. Not every business is built identical, and you'll likely find other beneficial campaigns for your clients. For now, though, I recommend considering the above types of campaigns as your primary forms of campaign creation using MailChimp.

4. Creating your campaign

With MailChimp, you'll have access to several different campaign styles to pick from. The most common one is your 'Regular' campaign: this is the campaign that enables the most effective change. You can design and customise it as you see fit, but you'll also get to choose from options including:

- **Regular.** The most common campaign type, and easily the most flexible. Allows you more or less total control over the content, layout and scheduling of messages.
- **Plain text.** These are text-only and remove all formatting options. Commonly used when targeting a senior audience, who are less likely to use HTML-friendly email.
- **A/B Testing.** Enables you to send more than one version of the same email to see which one comes out with the best results. Test these in different ways, from the time they are sent to variations of the heading or the content itself.
- **Automated.** These are useful for sending things like welcome messages to new subscribers, and to help get everyone up-to-speed as soon as they join. Great for starting a new email chain with individuals as soon as they sign up, without re-sending old emails to current subscribers.

You can also create different campaigns to run concurrently with relative ease when using MailChimp, thanks to the development of landing pages within your account. This is great for promoting your professional services further and will help with building more leads to make each campaign more effective.

To start off with, once you choose the style of campaign you wish to create (I suggest initially sticking with Regular), begin adding in the recipients, the subject matter and even the email design. As you complete the key parts needed for your email to send, they'll be ticked off on the checklist provided.

To determine who to send the email to, either add in individuals or pick a distinct group within your list. Select everyone you wish to send this campaign to. You can even pick different segments, such as inactive subscribers or specific subscribers within that group. Be sure to tick "Personalise the 'To' field", too – this makes sure their name is used, instead of their email address, making it feel more personal. Personalised emails help with your conversion rates due to higher engagement levels.

For the subject title of the email you have 150 characters to play with, so make this as appealing as possible to encourage subscribers to click into the full email. Think about who you are targeting, and why you want to target them, and build the title around that – a question often works well at this stage.

Next, you will need to click on 'Design Email'; within the Campaign Builder. When you do that, pick from a series of templates which MailChimp comes with. From the layout of the letter to the kind of theme, you'll have all sorts of styles to choose from. When you get more experienced, you could even use the 'code your own' function to produce something unique to your business.

For now, I recommend just building your campaigns as normal using the designs you start with. Lastly, hit the Preview and Test section, and see how the email looks on various platforms – including mobile. Also check any links within the email to ensure they are valid. I would suggest sending test emails to yourself first to get a clear idea of how the email template looks and feels before sending it out to clients. This way if you are not happy with anything, it will give you the chance to modify and improve the email until you are content.

Now you are done setting up the campaign, it's important you pay attention to tracking its performance accordingly. Be sure to check in the 'Settings and Tracking' section of your campaign manager that the tracking feature is switched on.

5. Measuring results of your campaigns

Lastly, you have to pay attention to the quality of your results. Once your email campaign is up and running, you should track how it's performing and measure your outcomes. Email campaigns run on MailChimp will provide you with vital data including the number of clicks, your open rate, social activity on your email and various other key factors.

Simply click on the 'Reports' page within your MailChimp account and view the metrics for each campaign you run. The Overview page breaks down essential data, including the number of recipients and the number of clicks you've had. You'll also get crucial measures like bounce rates and the number of people who may have opted out by unsubscribing, which you will need to know and pay close attention to.

You'll also get 24-hour performance graphs, social media shares and the number of links that were clicked – and how many times per link. It's all very informative and should make tracking and improving your campaigns a far less challenging, fraught experience.

Tap into the various tabs within, such as Activity and Links, to delve into more detailed analysis than the Overview provides. This should really help to speed up the process of refinement and make it easier for you to get the results you want.

Yes, you will need to act on these metrics, and, yes, you will need to take risks. If something is not working, though, the analysis found in the Reports page will be essential to your long-term success. While it does take good analytical skills to determine what MailChimp is suggesting, you should be able to act on the data it provides. From this you can distinguish if you need to make a telling improvement to each campaign.

Email Marketing and GDPR

Before we call it quits with email, I think it's necessary you take the time to look at a significant piece of EU legislation around email subscription lists and handling personal data. It was introduced in 2018 and has become a major topic of conversation across internet marketing.

It's known as the General Data Protection Regulation (GDPR) and is something every modern business needs to get to grips with. For one, it's changed just how blasé you can be about how you use your clients' personal data. Before the May 2018 implementation of GDPR, you could more or less do as you liked with clients' email addresses, contact data and other personal details supplied by them.

It made building an email marketing campaign much easier. At the same time, though, GDPR is useful. Why? Because now you know that anyone who receives your message has given you explicit permission to contact them, thus, showing their interest in what you have to say. GDPR states you should only collect the personal data you intend to use. Therefore, your business will probably ask for fewer personal details. Consequently, you're much more likely to benefit from higher conversion rates. If subscribers don't need to provide too much personal information, they are more likely to fill out your marketing forms and convert from a prospect into a lead.

Now, most of those people who have made their living with email marketing and were used to the old way of handling personal data may not be particularly fond of GDPR. In fact, they might fear it's going to decimate their mailing lists and make it much harder to sell anything. However, with the consequence potentially being a fine as large as €20m or 4% of your global turnover, whichever is higher, if you fall foul of the regulations, you must play by the rules.

How GDPR Impacts on Email Marketing

The best thing to do at this point would be to check out the main GDPR regulations. A good source of this can be found on The Law Society's website, www.lawsociety.org.uk, which has a section dedicated to GDPR. You are required to be much more careful with personal data, and you will have to make sure you take care in protecting, securing and storing all such data moving forward. If you don't have any email subscribers at present, you may not need to worry about this too much yet. **If you do have subscribers, you must contact them and re-gain their permission to hold their data**. Starting from May 2018, anyone who joins up is giving you permission to message them, **as long as they explicitly choose to opt in to your marketing emails.**

The biggest change is where you have any kind of tick box which says something like 'I would love to subscribe to updates from COMPANY', then **that box must be displayed as unticked by default. The user must choose to tick the box themselves.**

Additionally, you are no longer permitted to have a blanket term which says something like 'You agree to our Terms and Privacy Policy by signing up'. You must provide a tick box for agreeing to the terms, asking individuals to both actively accept emails and confirm acceptance of your terms. You can't assume someone agrees by default, which would then require them to opt out if they are not interested or in agreement.

There is a lot more to GDPR than I can cover here, but I'd suggest you consider bringing a professional compliance officer into your firm if you intend on marketing to any clients in the EU, or even work with a single person based in the EU. Where you are at all unsure about GDPR rules and requirements it's best to get expert advice from a legal professional before you send out any emails for marketing purposes.

Webinars

I would highly recommend utilising webinars as a lead generation strategy and to increase your bottom-line profits. Webinars are simply the online equivalent of seminars, only they are hosted on the internet. People log in to listen to you, similar to a video conference connection, although you are the only speaker. As with any other presentation you make, webinars allow you to build authority, share expertise and give the audience some advice which they could benefit from.

For example, as an accountant you may choose to run a webinar on helping people to file their Self-Assessment forms. This would give you the chance to educate your audience, throw in some awesome value and make them realise just how worthwhile a little knowledge can be when it comes to accountancy or tax matters. The more you show others how to do the mundane stuff for themselves, which you would rather avoid taking on, the less likely they are to need you for that service. They will be more appreciative of the expertise you provide on more advanced and challenging accountancy issues.

Why You Need to Start Running Webinars

The main reason why you should start running webinars is to build your authority and increase exposure, but it also helps you get ahead of your competition. Professional services firms are often quite aloof when it comes to sharing information. This can make it tough for you to start using webinars because you may have to overcome a preconceived idea that you won't be providing anything worth paying attention too. This isn't the case, though: **most of the time, your competitor is simply ignoring a goldmine.**

You could run webinars purely on the basis that it enables you to give out valuable information to your audience. If you would like to spend more time on lucrative specialist tax solutions, then running webinars on anything from submitting tax returns to treatment of expenses for entertaining staff and clients could bring you a significant return on the time invested here.

Webinars are a great way of generating new leads too. Since people log into webinar sessions eager to learn something new on a topic, they are likely to be hot prospects. As long as your content engages them, they will probably continue seeking more answers or solutions from you afterwards. It's the perfect way to show your audience what you are able to do and how much you know.

You could even use webinars to help promote other parts of your business such as events and workshops, as some people might appreciate learning from you in person rather than through the web. For others, the time and travel commitment involved in a live meet up is too much, so educating them in the comfort of their own home may have more appeal.

If people want a more face-to-face experience, then invite them to visit your Eventbrite pages, encouraging them to sign up for more of your guidance in due course. I'll touch on events shortly, but this can be extremely effective for you as a lead generation tactic, for both your business and gaining a new audience for live events you want to host.

A client of mine, an accounting firm in Greater London, is attracting new guests just this way, very effectively. They are using webinars to educate prospects and then encouraging them to attend live workshops for Making Tax Digital (MTD). They are achieving a consistent conversion rate of 70% which is phenomenal. I don't know many other firms that are achieving this kind of success rate.

Whatever methods you use to educate and inform your readership, the more they recognise new ways you can help them. Webinars are also very convenient because you operate these through your PC at home or in the office. So long as you have a screen capture system and invest in a recording tool to pick up your voice, maybe a webcam so they can see your face too, you are ready to get started. Since it's so easy to set up and stream, you could even do it through YouTube, so you should really get to work on them immediately.

Running a webinar is a cost-effective exercise which gives your business another great opportunity to capture quality leads. Due to the low cost of the tools needed to run one, it offers a potentially significant return on investment when done right.

How Can You Make Sure Your Webinar is Visible?

Setting up and running a webinar is simple, using anything from ON24, GoToWebinar, Webex, Adobe Connect, or even YouTube. Spreading awareness about your webinars to gain the right audience may prove hard, initially. Of course, you can always combine this with the use of your email marketing campaigns, encouraging those who are already subscribed to your email service to take part. Email marketing will help you massively here if you have a growing list of contacts who like what you do.

If they are already using your email content to learn from you, chances are they will appreciate the invitation to one of your live web sessions. An email invite is going to help you get existing clients to join your webinars on top of promoting yourself in various ways to new prospects.

How then, can you ensure your webinar is visible to as many of your ideal clients as possible? Let's take a look at some ideas:

- **Guest Posts.** One of the best techniques, I believe, is to use guest posts to help you promote yourself. By having a recognised name in your industry post an article you have written on their site, you could then advertise to a much wider and relevant audience. An example of a guest post could be having your article being included on a website such as AccountingWEB, with your name and firm displayed there.
- **Blog Posts.** Sharing the content on your own website and blogging about the upcoming webinar is useful too. It catches the attention of those who already follow you and have an interest, meaning they may want to take part and invite others. They might also promote you on their social media and to their own contacts.
- **Social Media.** Of course, you should post on all your social media channels advertising the webinar. A promotion message or two each day in the run-up to the webinar is bound to attract some regular followers, and some new clients, making it a must-use strategy.
- **LinkedIn.** Probably the best tool outside of guest posting, or even more so if you use social media a lot, is LinkedIn. It generates so many interested leads. Simply look for a group you are part of and ask the group owner for permission to promote the webinar there.

- **Events.** Through the use of Facebook and LinkedIn events options you should be able to promote the webinar to as many connections as you have. This is a great way to ensure you build your audience by expanding your network, and hopefully increasing conversions.

NICK'S TIPS

Document your entire webinar process. Create a calendar, as you'll need to trial and test different variations to identify where your best conversion rates are. Plan them weeks in advance to ensure every stage of the webinar is in top shape. Try to keep records for each webinar format that you undertake: over time, you'll work out what kind of webinars your audience appreciate the most.

Podcasting

Podcasting is also another means of reaching large audiences without a tremendous amount of effort. However, let me be clear when I say **podcasting for a professional service such as accountancy is tough.** There aren't many people doing it and for good reason: it's hard to get the tone right. Done with care though, podcasting could become an exceptional choice of tool for you to work with.

If you are wondering what a podcast is, in the strictest sense it's an audio file which is made available online to download or stream. It's normally a series of content, with regular guests who talk about important subjects within your industry. You could use your podcast to cover everything from accountancy news, to tips and tricks for your listeners to learn from. I would suggest you try and bring in a fellow accountant to help you with the podcast: two expert minds are much more likely to be of benefit than one. If you can't find someone to help, though, going solo can still be effective.

Why Podcasting Makes Sense for the Passionate Professional

- For one, it's not an isolated format any longer. There are over half a million podcasts out there, with many more made available for streaming regularly.
- While most people associate podcasts with things like sport and history, business is the second largest sector for podcasting.
- There are over 50 awesome accountancy podcasts, coming from the likes of TED Talks and Accounting Today. This should show you that a relevant podcast isn't a flash in the pan idea.
- It doesn't require a huge amount of investment to build up a quality podcast, as you only need good quality recording software and some time to spend editing.
- Few other forms of media allow you to display to others your command of accountancy delivered in such a convenient and relaxed way.
- You can give out great tips and educate your listeners, even bringing in other accountancy experts to add authority and visibility to the podcast and your business.
- Podcasts should be kept reasonably short: a 30-minute episode is usually more than enough to cover what you need to, all without boring your listeners.
- This is another form of media that can be easily optimised to help improve your search engine ranking, whilst bringing in new listeners, and, eventually, clients.

How to Create a Quality Podcast

To begin podcasting you usually only need to have the basics, like a laptop and a microphone. You could even do this on a smartphone if you wish, most people start out in podcast productions just using their existing equipment to record on. Some subtle professional touches can really help take this to the next level. Firstly, you have to find places to upload your podcast to and you can't just turn to Spotify iTunes. I recommend you look at Libsyn as a platform to launch them on.

The simple reason is that Libsyn is more cost-effective and will ensure your podcast is shared across all key distribution panels. This will help you to get your podcast noticed, it will also mean you get a copy of the link to your podcast to upload directly onto your website.

When first starting out, you'll want to try and get it listed on key places like Acast, Spreaker, iTunes, Spotify and Stitcher. Each time you produce a new episode be sure to notify people of its release via all your platforms. Write a blog post about it, create social media posts and, of course, send an email to all your subscribers.

Here are some musts if you want to create a good quality podcast:

- A good, quiet place to record in, with strong acoustics. Look for anything which might constitute background noise and try to do what you can to stamp it out.

- Invest in a good quality microphone, too. Most people use their smartphone, but it can be needlessly sensitive. There are quality microphones available around the £50-100 mark.

- Get good quality earphones for the editing side of things too. You'll easily find quality earphones for picking up problems with the sound at around £50-70, give or take.

- You may want to get your hands-on worthwhile audio software, there are several free choices. If you own an Apple iPad then you'll probably have GarageBand free with it, which is a good option. Alternatively, you could download a tool called Audacity, though it can be a little confusing for the layman. If you find the mixing and editing side of podcasting not something you want to take on yourself, consider outsourcing it to a professional.

- Invest in getting a quality producer. There are reliable professional experts to choose from on good freelance websites for affordable fees. This is great for making sure you get your podcast properly mastered, edited, uploaded and syndicated to major outlets, like I mentioned before.

Finally, you may want to play a few bars of music at the start of the podcast, as an introduction of sorts. I won't insult your intelligence, but please remember to check it out for fair use: you don't want to attract the ire of someone who believes you used their content in poor faith.

Also, if you are explaining a more complex tax or legal issue, or an area of compliance, you have to be very particular about this so that everything is made clear to the listener. Keep this in mind, and you can make most episodes a means of lead generation, trust building and authority development.

Events

The last and probably the most effective strategy in conjunction with webinars and email marketing is running live events. These are locally held workshops you host, where the reputational benefits and trust building that come from them can be invaluable. **People who come along to one of your workshops will be there to learn, so you need to be ready to put together a high-quality talk which delivers great value.**

Event management and delivery is tough and for someone without presentation skills or the confidence needed to talk in front of an audience, this can seem daunting. A workshop or event is a live-action version of running a webinar, with the difference being these have a localised appeal, and you have people right in front of you to answer to. **However, the significant advantage with running live events is that, for the most part, you will be the only accountant in your area doing this.**

For some reason, despite being a brilliant method for trust building, marketing and networking, many professionals disregard running events as a worthwhile marketing solution. Make sure you don't fall into this category! Instead be a pro-active, forward thinking firm that leads by example. If you're not going to do anything else, run events. Trust me when I tell you they will impact your bottom line significantly with high-quality clients. As I mentioned earlier, there are a few firms out there that are making the most of running workshops in their local areas and they are achieving great results.

NICK'S TIPS

Remember you don't physically need to be there yourself to run workshops. It's possible to hire someone to give a talk or use your employees to represent your firm instead. They may be more excited and comfortable in doing so, and it shows you appreciate their skills and capabilities. If you aren't someone who likes to stand up and talk in front of a large crowd, it's going to benefit you more to have someone else do so on your behalf.

Why Running Events Makes Sense as a Professional

- For one, it allows you to dive deeply into selected topics. Let's say you are an expert in Research & Development issues, or you are a specialist in Making Tax Digital. You could run a live event to advise businesses on how to benefit from tax reliefs or be ready for new rules.
- Online marketing is very powerful indeed, but few things are quite so enticing to a potential client than seeing you live in action when you are showcasing your skills and interacting with them. It marks you as a leader and someone who can understand their industry from an expert perspective.

- It's a great way to connect with locals, building trust in what you do and the ways you could help them to improve their operations. Many smaller professional firms find a lot of their clientele is drawn in from their nearby business community.

- It can also draw the attention of local media which gives you great public relations exposure. Issue a press release to local journalists and invite them to attend.

- Putting on an event shows you are willing to go that little bit further to support your fellow professionals in their roles and that you care about their long-term success.

- Of course, the other major benefit of running an event is how the personal interaction makes it easier to gain some extra sales, creating awareness of all the different services you provide to local businesses.

- Networking is beneficial here, too. Those who attend the event are likely to see how you are able to help them out, and they come primed with a degree of interest on your subject matter, but equally, they may know others who might need the same. This makes it a great way to gain some new contacts and clients.

- Also, you can use this event to introduce other specialist services which you offer after the event. This is likely to help attendees recognise other ways you are able to support them aside from what was discussed at the event, making you seem even more attractive as an advisor.

How to Make Your Event a Success

Firstly, you must decide when to host your event. Hosting it at the right time is crucial. For example, hosting a Self-Assessment workshop on the 1st February would not be much use. Instead, timing it for early January, or better yet, sometime in the early winter (October, November) can ensure you get maximum exposure to those individuals who need relevant advice.

Then, you should find a local venue that is affordable. Picking somewhere with good lighting, comfortable seating and easy room-wide views of key peripherals like the projector screen is essential. Since people are giving up their time to come to this event, it must be both a suitable location and an event that delivers something worthwhile.

Of course, you could host the event at your own or even from a client's premises, if the location, space and features are all appropriate for this. Using a client's premises can give you greater geographic reach to target new audiences and make some extra sales. You could even have a partnership arrangement with the client in question meaning both parties could benefit from the event publicity.

Before holding your event, consider these questions carefully. *Is what you are offering via a talk/presentation worthwhile and useful? Or is the talk only a part of an event's activities, mixed with some social engagement and networking?*

Before the invitations are sent out, you should have the details and content mapped out, as well as what outcome you would like from it:

a) what your ambition is for the event and,

b) what kind of action you expect those who come along to take.

Do you want them to contact you soon after for help? Or do you want to help them be more self-sustainable when it comes to their finances, leveraging your expertise to market your professional services to those who need more complex solutions or specific advice?

It's a tough thing to answer, but you have to bear this in mind as it will determine the theme of the event and, therefore, the outcome. An event which is looking to push your services should see a high return from attendees taking upsold services. For those where you are looking to build trust and authority, you should hopefully receive more enquiries from other people saying they were referred by an attendee.

Remember there is a cost for the event itself. You may also need to pay for food and beverages. I recommend contacting local catering services or seeing what kind of services the venue can lay on.

As well as trying to find a venue which is in a good place in your town or city, I suggest you think carefully about the time of the event too. Try to find a timeframe that suits most people. Consider whether you should cover only one or two topics, or have a full day of talks, presentations and lectures. Also bear in mind how much knowledge anyone can absorb on a subject. You don't want your audience to get bored or switch off; the human brain can only take in so much information at any one time. Typically, the end of the day is a good choice for one which focuses on a particular topic, especially where it will draw a larger audience. Although the beginning of the day can appeal to professionals looking to learn about more complex subjects that may require higher levels of participation and engagement.

With regards to choosing a day, aiming for mid-week or towards the latter end of the week is recommended as most people will have cleared the bulk of their weekly routine tasks by then. Attendees may feel they would get more value learning from you than by working in their offices that particular day. My most profitable workshops are on Wednesdays and Thursdays compared to those held at the start of a week. On a Friday people are more distracted as they organise their weekend activities. So be sure to consider this when planning to run your own workshop/event.

Gauging Numbers & Sending Invites

You should have an idea of approximately how many attendees you want to invite, as this will determine the venue choice. If you think you are going to have a big turnout, you need to try and find an open space with good acoustics so your voice can carry. Where it's likely to be a smaller event though, try to avoid anywhere that might feel too tight or awkward.

If you want to get people to come along, then you should set up event notifications on all your social media channels and post or blog about it. Send out your invites at least one month prior to the date. Try to give advance notice of maybe two months, preferably ten weeks.

Make it clear where the event will be held, why they should come along and any benefits they will gain from it. Also, try to request RSVPs from your potential attendees at least a week before the event date to ensure everything is properly arranged.

Don't just presume you have a fully booked venue because you have received a lot of general interest and enquiries. Be sure to expect around 25% of those who enquired or signed up not to arrive on the day. I'd recommend you try and get a more accurate reading by making it easy for anyone to contact you on social media or by phone, informing you if they cannot make it.

Seeing a Return on Investment

Since running an event could cost you anything up to a few thousand pounds to organise (maybe even more depending on your venue and your location), it's important to know whether it has been well received and could lead to new business. If possible, introduce yourself around before the talk and be available afterwards to answer any questions. This will be key as you'll find people approaching you after the workshop or event is over to find out more. View each person who talks to you as a potential client, some will sign up there and then, others may take some more time to convert. Hopefully, you will have covered your costs from new business signed up on the day.

Be sure you don't lose any momentum generated from the event to maximise your ROI. You should follow up with all attendees. How to do that is simple: create an email campaign to message everyone who came, around 24 hours after attendance. Split this into three separate content options: firstly, a thank you and welcome one to those who came and signed up to your services, secondly a thank you and a sign up offer reminder or an invitation to book a one-to-one call for those close to converting, and thirdly a thank you along with details of the next planned event to go out to existing clients and other regular attendees. Remember you can automate this whole process, as mentioned earlier.

You could offer a slight discount or some kind of payment plan to those prospects who are close to buying but are slightly more price sensitive. Personally, I tend to avoid this but at times you may feel it's worthwhile to maximise sales conversions, especially if you didn't hit the level of expected sales on the day of the event itself. If you've provided enough value though, you should not have to consider this, as sales will increase from growing your audience.

Make sure you always follow up as much as possible after hosting each event, responding at least with a thank you to every attendee. It's key to maximising an event's success and adding to your bottom-line profits in the future.

Now you know about some of the other ways to increase awareness and authority, it's time to look at the last chapter, which is focused on measuring performance. It's all well and good carrying out these techniques, but how do you know if they are benefiting your business?

Takeaways

- Your reputation as a business can be enhanced when you are visible on more than one form of online media.
- Email marketing campaigns are the best way to cross-pollinate your social media promotional activities, expanding your network through making the most of the 'big five' platforms.
- Consider running webinars, podcasts, workshops and events as they are a great way to build trust with clients at a relatively low cost.
- Invest properly in good quality equipment for any audio or visual recording and editing, these are part of a long-term strategy.
- Hosting live events in your area can really help you to drive local business to you, although, as before, make sure the venue, catering and other facilities are all up to scratch.

CHAPTER 12

METRICS MATTER: MEASURING YOUR MARKETING EFFORTS

So far I have I covered various ways that could add to your toolkit and give more visibility to your professional services. These are a great series of extra strategies you could easily use to your advantage. However, just like any other kind of marketing, it will take some time to figure out where your best results come from. Speaking of which, how do you *know* if your marketing is doing your business any good?

For those who know me, you'll already appreciate that I value statistics above just about anything else. I suppose this comes from my financial background, having worked in reporting teams for large corporate companies previously. Everything needs to be calculated, measured and looked at closely. If you're not aware of the statistics to measure marketing outcomes and what Key Performance Indicators (KPI's) to keep an eye on, how are you supposed to improve and optimise your marketing campaign? The number of marketers I have had conversations with that simply don't understand the importance of KPI's is flabbergasting.

Statistics don't lie and once you recognise the importance of KPI's, you'll soon be able to manage and direct your marketing in a more effective manner. In this final chapter then, I want to show you the importance of having useful metrics put in place. By helping you to more accurately track and measure your KPIs, you'll be in the best possible position to help your business thrive. I'm also going to help you use a tool that's been mentioned a few times previously and is essential to your success: Google Analytics.

KPI's are Key

Most people will be familiar with the more common KPIs, the usual suspects like sales, cost per lead (CPL), conversion rates and of course, customer lifetime value (LTV). These are the top-level statistics which measure the successfulness of a campaign's main objective or goal.

Sales is self-explanatory, measured as the amount of revenue your inbound marketing campaign has brought in for your company. It's vital to know this to understand how effective your marketing campaign is. If a campaign isn't generating the desired revenue it may be worth redirecting the spend on it elsewhere.

Typically, your cost per lead is something you need to consider. If your leads are going to be costing you more to gain and convert than they bring in, then you naturally need to make a change. Calculating the cost per lead can be a little confusing, as it requires you to integrate all your marketing automation and CRM platforms, as well as ensuring your associated costs are considered. Once you know the costs that are involved in both inbound and outbound marketing, you'll get a good idea of how much you are spending to bring in new clients, giving you greater insight into what you have to work and improve upon.

Conversion rates are slightly easier to manage and amount to the number of people who actually wind up either providing you with their contact details or making a purchase. If your landing page has a low conversion rate, but lots of traffic, then it means you are halfway there. You should probably look to make small adjustments over time, thinking about where to add more value. You may want to refer back to Chapter 4 to remind yourself of some of the tactics covered there.

Your customer lifetime value (LTV) should also be considered because it's about determining the long-term worth of each client for your business. You want every client to help you earn additional revenues, but it's obvious that some clients will be more valuable to you than others. Remember the Pareto Principle?

The simplest way to determine your customer lifetime value is by thinking about the annual revenue per client multiplied by the average customer lifespan (customer relationship in years), minus the initial cost of acquiring them. It's advantageous to know what this is for your firm so you can concentrate your efforts on acquiring your most ideal and profitable clients, focusing your lead nurturing campaigns on those who fit your ideal client profile.

The most important metric though, is Return on Investment, or ROI. If you are going to excel as a business, you'll need to aim to generate a high ROI from your marketing activities.

I've only touched on these common KPI's briefly as they are quite generic in my opinion. While it's good to be made aware of them, I'd like to delve into more specific metrics which I believe tell you more about your online marketing performance. Ones you'll find most interesting and are concrete evidence of the success you should be seeing from your work so far. Of course, if you'd like to know more about the KPI's mentioned here, there are plenty of articles online to search out which talk about the metrics above at great length. With the following metrics though, you can really make a huge difference to your professional firm by appreciating their relevance and maximising their value.

What Key Metrics Should You Track and Measure?

It's important to note that the first six of these metrics are, for the most part, essential to achieving success with Google Analytics. I'll break down that side of things shortly, but the most important metrics to track would be:

- **Quality of leads.** This is essentially the fit of each to your ideal client: how likely is it that the lead you have received will be interested in what you have to offer?
- **Sales Conversion.** Arguably the most important metric. How many sales are you getting? How many actual purchases or new clients have you achieved from your campaigns?

- **Traffic level.** How many people are coming to visit your website in the first place? Getting to grips with this metric and what insights it gives is obviously important: the more visitors, the merrier, generally.
- **Website engagement.** However, traffic is only beneficial if it shows a good pattern in website engagement, which pages visitors view, and the time spent looking at different content. If people are leaving without engaging something is wrong.
- **Social Media ROI.** Your return on investment for social media marketing should be reviewed regularly, as it will help you quickly determine how campaigns on each of the platforms are progressing.
- **SEO ROI.** The success of the steps put in place in Chapter 7 and beyond: what kind of success are you actually seeing from the work you put into optimisation?
- **Pay-per-click ads.** Can be tracked in various ways using tracking links as well as several analytics tools. Simply head into the Google Ads campaign manager and take a look at the numbers. Track the number of calls derived from your ads or website too.
- **Email open rates.** Most tools you will use for email marketing, such as those mentioned in Chapter 11, MailChimp and aWeber, can provide you with this tracking data.
- **Authority level.** Using platforms such as Eventbrite, you can easily track your events and find out how successful they are. Podcasts are tracked using download volumes, also the number of downloads per unique IP address, while webinars can be tracked using tools like WorkCast.

So, now you know what the key metrics to review are, let's look at how you can use the data to your advantage. Why does this even matter?

EXERCISE

Write down a list of some KPI's you consider as being key ones to your business that are not listed above. Think about how you are measuring these KPI's currently and what changes you might make to improve your results.

Why You Need to Measure Your Marketing Metrics

Put simply, you are not making the most of your budget if you don't know which marketing strategies are working in your favour. In a way, it would be like placing an advertisement for your business in a local newspaper but never actually bothering to check how many people were referred to you via the advert. It's blind marketing, and basically means you have no guidance on where you could improve or otherwise strengthen your message.

A client of mine, an accounting firm in North London, had been using some offline marketing methods to try to acquire new business for their personal tax division. While I am still a fan of offline marketing, there isn't much value to sticking with it if you're not going to track and measure the effectiveness of the campaign – offline or not!

My client had distributed 5000 leaflets in the local area. When I asked the question, *'how many leads or calls did you receive?'* they couldn't give me an accurate answer. This was because there was no system in place to identify which leads came from their website ordinarily or which were in response to a leaflet. Now we can probably assume 10% of people who received a leaflet followed up by making an enquiry and only 10% of those enquiries turned into new clients, but without accurately tracking the campaign it's just going in blind without any strategic focus.

Once my team implemented a call tracking feature, we were able to eliminate this flaw and ascertain whether the offline marketing spend was worthwhile or not. By including a simple virtual telephone number as well as a separate email address (not the standard company email address) on the leaflet, we could calculate the cost of acquisition for the few clients who came on board. More importantly, we were able to recognise the return on investment was not high enough and concluded it was much better to redirect that marketing spend on PPC instead. You need to see proof in the performance of anything you do, especially if you have a limited marketing budget.

The other reason why you should be investigating and routinely reviewing your metrics is that you have no reason *not* to. With so many easy to use tracking tools available for digging into metrics and determining the effectiveness of any campaign, the list of legitimate excuses you can use is thin indeed.

You have to be able to understand how to both track and analyse these key factors above, not least the fact that this ties in directly with what was mentioned in Chapter 3. Your business needs goals, but it needs to have goals which are measurable and compare objectives against actual performance. It's the only way to truly know if the outcomes are achieved as a consequence of your marketing efforts. If your goal is to increase engagement on your website, then you will need to measure your SEO success by looking at your SEO ROI metric. If it's to attract better quality leads, then you'll need to pay more attention to metrics that help you assess the quality of leads for your business.

If you simply just have a generic goal in mind, such as *'I want to have more cash in the bank',* then it will be much harder to work towards achieving as it's simply not specific enough. The campaign that matters for your firm will be based on your stage of growth, your industry, the level of competition and your personal ambitions. However, any marketing campaign you run must be built around something you can measure to see its success. There is no real benefit to simply running generic campaigns, as it can make it hard to see if they meet a specific goal. As mentioned previously, campaigns fall into three main categories, Attainment, Monetisation and Interaction. To measure the desired objective from each of these types you should look at the metric that fits the relevant outcome of it, and whether each one is giving an adequate ROI.

You must measure every campaign properly, because it's the only way to know if each campaign is

a) working and,

b) suitable for your business.

When it comes to measuring your pay-per-click ads, for example, it's important to know *why* they are doing well, or not so well, and what refinements you could make to ensure greater success. Otherwise, you are essentially running on hope. By using the little bit of code provided to you when running your Google PPC campaigns, you should be able to start seeing some results fairly quickly. These might not be exactly what you require to begin with, but you can easily overcome that.

When you install your email marketing platform of choice for your campaigns, more or less any tool worth its salt will give you access to a host of analytical statistics. One of the most important metrics from this, though, is the email opening rate. If you aren't seeing a good opening rate, then you need to adjust your campaign. If you never looked at your email opening rate, would you even know if your campaigns were failing? Just the smallest of tweaks, for example changing the subject line to make it more compelling, can make all the difference to your email opening rates.

The reason why you should try and measure your authority or exposure level is quite simple: you need to know that your efforts are not in vain. If you want to be able to develop further proof of your own success to entice new clients, you have to show some evidence as to why they can put their trust in you. It's vital you give yourself every opportunity to see what must change, because the results you receive back will inform you of how much or how little work is still required to continue on the right path.

The same goes for your events, your podcasts and your webinars. Each one can be tracked using the software which allows you to manage, run or distribute them. Most of the good podcast syndication tools come with analytical software, as do a whole host of webinar hosting programs. I made some suggestions in the last chapter about the different software you could use for each, although for events I'd recommend Eventbrite. It offers analytical tracking links which can be used to ascertain how many visits, clicks and ticket sales were made, along with the number of attendees versus invites sent.

So, now you know why you should pay attention to these three metrics, let's go back a bit. I mentioned six other key metrics above, which all play a significant role in measuring your marketing success; quality of leads, sales conversion, traffic level, website engagement, social media ROI and SEO ROI. What is the best way to analyse and track all of them? Google Analytics.

Let's look at why that is.

Using Google Analytics

I've mentioned this a few times throughout the book. Google Analytics is basically the statistical tracking and measuring arm of the Google empire. It's the one which delivers a painstaking amount of data to you, time and time again. Google Analytics is among your most informative and insightful tools. It's a simple to use system that Google offers, allowing you to investigate all the key metrics mentioned here, as well as other important metrics, to ascertain how well you are performing, or not performing, as the case may be.

While drawing conclusions from what Google Analytics indicates can be tough, it's by no means an impossibility. These metrics guide you to making more intelligent choices, empowering you to understand not only **what, and why something is working for you,** but more importantly **what isn't and what could be improved.** To find out how to read into metrics you'll need to first have a Google Analytics account set up, if you haven't got one already. How do you sign up to it?

Setting up a Google Analytics Account

1. Start off by heading over to google.com/analytics. Once you are there, you'll be asked to create your account. Do this by clicking the 'Start for Free' button.

2. You should be able sign in with your normal Google credentials, or create a new login from scratch. I recommend just linking this new account to your normal business Google account.

3. Now, you need to set up an 'account' name. Each 'account' is the highest level of your company. This will just be your business name, e.g. Joe Bloggs Accountancy. Within the account you can then designate different 'properties' to be analysed. Each digital platform, such as a website or app will be classed as a 'property' and will come with a different tracking code.

4. Set up a 'property' for your Google Analytics account: this is going to be your website address, so feel free to put that in. If you have more than one website, you would need to create multiple properties.

5. Properties are good for setting up specific metrics. You could, for example, split analytics drawn from your blog from those of your About pages and separate the measures by country, if you work internationally.

6. Choose your details with regards to the Industry Category for your firm, and then the Reporting Time Zone, presuming you are in the UK you'll want to choose GMT.

7. Once you complete all of this, you will see a button called 'Get Tracking ID' so click that. From there you need to read and accept the terms of the service agreement which appears.

8. You'll need to highlight the section under your Tracking ID that begins with <script> and ends with </script> - copy it as you need to add it in to your website or have someone do it for you.

9. Most website templates require you to place this right at the very bottom of your website code. Try and place it right before the closing tag. A closing tag in coding begins with </> so look for something that ends with </> like the </script> above.

Now you have installed this code, one way or the other, it's time to test it out. Do this by visiting the website on your home or office PC browser, on your smartphone and on any other devices you can get access to. Then, head on over to the Google Analytics dashboard.

Here, click on the 'Real Time' section, and go to 'Overview'. You should see the real-time section data and, if you have done it right, several active users will be listed which correspond to your own number of uses. If it has not worked then you'll need to follow the above steps again or reach out to someone for help.

You aren't out of the woods yet though! Now you need to set up Conversion Tracking. To do this go to Google Analytics Goals. Underneath User Management and above Content Grouping on the dashboard, look for Goals. In here, it's possible to set specific aims for each page. For example, if you have a page which thanks someone for signing up to your email list, you could use the URL of that thank you page and assign any visitor who arrives there as a conversion.

It's a bit challenging but you should get there soon enough. You just need a bit of practice.

How to Measure the Most Important Metrics

Now your Google Analytics account is live and kicking, it's time to start measuring the six key metrics or KPIs which matter to your firm. How do you do that? It's quite simple, once you get the hang of it!

NICK'S TIPS

I would recommend checking these metrics from your desktop PC or laptop rather than a mobile device, as a bigger screen here will be much easier for you to view and navigate these key metrics.

Quality of Leads

For you to acquire more ideal clients you need to draw in the right visitors to your website, the ones you want to see there. The best way to know if someone is genuinely interested in your services is by identifying their browsing habits. Seeing if they continue on to informative content onsite, spend some time on key pages and whether they head over to the Contact or Sign Up page to take action are all good indicators. Naturally, a high-quality lead is someone who is interested in what you have to offer. How do you track this?

Simply go to Google Analytics, and head on over to the Goals page. When you get to the Goals page, click on 'Visualisation' as displayed in Fig. 12.1.

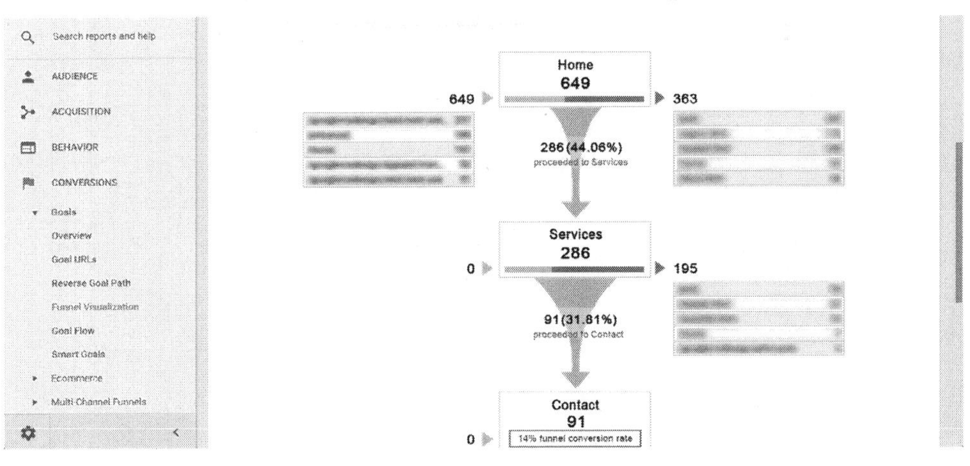

Figure 12.1

Here you are able to identify what pieces of content and what pages are converting people into leads. For example, someone who checks out your Services page should then follow-up with a move to pages such as your Contact Us page, indicating they are happy to work with you.

Typically, if you are seeing a lot of people either leave the site (high bounce rate) or not take much action, then you will be drawing in poor quality traffic. This means that your content isn't specific enough, and you are being too generic, particularly in the keyword selections used within your content. Similarly, if you are drawing in too many people who aren't looking for your services, getting quality leads will be a struggle.

Sales Conversion

More importantly you need to know whether the quality of lead metrics are translating into actual sales. To find out if this is happening, head on over to the Behaviour section of Google Analytics. Once there, click on 'Site Content', and then click onto 'All Pages' to see the details as per Fig. 12.2.

Figure 12.2

This shows you the average monetary value for each page of your website. The Page Value lets you know what pages are more actively contributing to sales, meaning you either need to:

a) reinforce these pages or,

b) work on improving the other pages to achieve a higher cross-site average.

Keep in mind that this only tracks single session conversions. As you know yourself, most people will look at your site, maybe view a competitor, and then return to make a decision later. Check the number of conversions from each channel, paid ads or organic traffic, using Assisted Conversions. This falls under the Conversions panel; simply click on 'Conversions', head on into 'Multi-Channel Funnels' and then 'Assisted Conversions'.

Be sure to use the Date Range tool, as displayed in Fig. 12.3. This helps you to determine which pieces of content should stay as part of the sales funnel, or if they might need to be updated, replaced or even removed. Use the checkbox to compare data for previous periods, specifying the data range as you wish. This helps you to see if there has been a performance drop-off from your business, or if certain pages are no longer performing due to lack of relevance etc.

Figure 12.3

Traffic Level

The level of website traffic is arguably your most important metric. Without any traffic, none of the other metrics really matter too much. To ascertain your traffic generating pages, all that you need to do is head on over to the Behaviour section of Google Analytics, and then head into Site Content and Landing Pages, shown in Fig. 12.4. You can see where people are landing on your website most commonly (it's going to show you the highest traffic pages by default, in chronological order).

Behavior
Overview
Behavior Flow
Site Content
All Pages
Content Drilldown
Landing Pages
Exit Pages
Site Speed
Site Search
Events

	Landing Page	Acquisition	
		Sessions	% New Sessions
		2,437 % of Total: 100.00% (2,437)	76.69% Avg for View: 76.69% (0.00%)
1.	/	886 (36.36%)	70.20%
2.	/services/accountancy/	136 (5.58%)	82.35%
3.	/services/taxation/	121 (4.97%)	86.78%
4.	/services/wealth management/	90 (3.69%)	68.89%
5.	/services/consultancy/	67 (2.75%)	80.60%
6.	/blog/how-employees-can-stay-motivated	65 (2.67%)	66.15%
7.	/blog/how-to-operate-your-start up-business	53 (2.17%)	69.81%

Figure 12.4

I would recommend drilling down into this a step further and paying attention to where your traffic is coming from, which is very handy to know. To check your landing page traffic sources, head into the Secondary Dimension drop down menu within this page, and then click on the Acquisition > Source/Medium option as seen in Fig. 12.5.

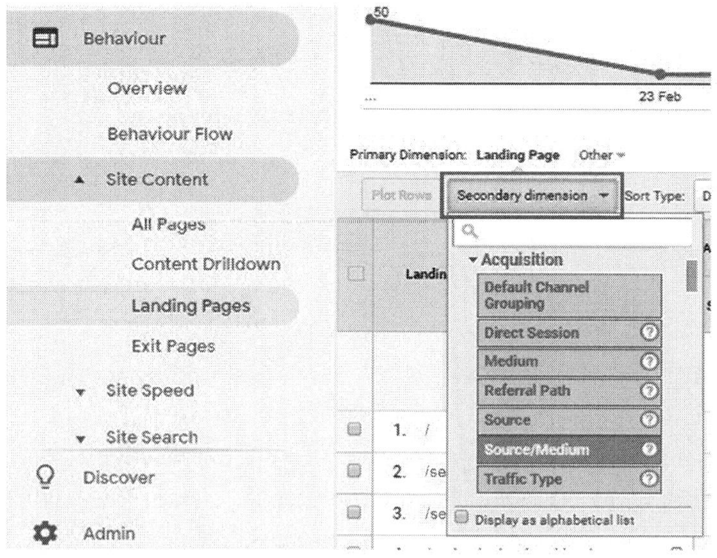

Figure 12.5

By knowing where your traffic stems from, you are able to understand where you need to focus, and re-focus, your marketing efforts. Is a visitor driven from direct traffic, organic traffic or paid traffic?

Landing Page	Source / Medium	Acquisition	
		Sessions	% New Sessions
		2,446 % of Total: 100.00% (2,446)	76.78% Avg for View: 76.78% (0.00%)
1. /	google / organic	275 (11.24%)	52.36%
2. /services/accountancy/	google / cpc	120 (4.91%)	89.17%
3. /services/taxation/	google / cpc	92 (3.76%)	89.13%
4. /services/wealth management/	google / cpc	57 (2.33%)	82.46%
5. /services/consultancy/	google / organic	42 (1.72%)	54.76%
6. /blog/how-employees-can-stay-motivated	linkedin.com / referral	40 (1.64%)	70.00%
7. /blog/how-to-operate-your-start up-business	facebook.com / referral	39 (1.59%)	76.92%

Figure 12.6

In this example, taken from one of my clients, you can clearly see that most of the traffic arriving at each of their landing pages is predominantly from Google as opposed to other social platforms. Again, this helps you see where your efforts should be most heavily concentrated. In this case, the metric indicates that it's worthwhile spending more time and effort on SEO and PPC to maximise conversions. LinkedIn efforts could also be improved here too, with more content creation added to drive LinkedIn connections to the website.

Website Engagement

The next metric you should inspect in detail indicates how people enjoy your website through their levels of engagement. It's all well and good visitors turning up, but if they aren't sticking around and engaging with your website content it will need some work done to improve it. The term used for people who turn up and then leave quickly is 'bounce rate'. The lower the bounce rate the better, in most cases. People might leave and then return later which is fair enough. It's the ones who leave and never return you have to focus on, providing content relevant to their searches.

If you see lots of people are arriving on your most popular blog post but leaving shortly after, it's not doing its intended job. Where it shows people are hanging around for a few minutes and then maybe visiting other pages, taking action, or even subscribing to your email list, you are doing well in terms of engagement.

To view your website engagement level simply go into the Audience section of Google Analytics, and then click on Overview as seen in Fig. 12.7. This tells you exactly what your bounce rate is, as well as things like how many pages are visited per session, or how many users have made up those sessions. It also tells you a vital statistic: the average duration of a session. If this is low, it means people are leaving quickly. After all, the more engaged someone is, logic dictates the longer they will stay around and explore other pages too.

Figure 12.7

I suggest you pay attention to the bottom three statistics; pages per session, average session duration and bounce rate. The data here for my client looks pretty good at first glance, as the bounce rate is relatively low, average session duration is adequate and the pages per session is reasonable.

Drill down further into the bounce rate metric to see what it is for specific pieces of content and pages on your site. Just check the Behaviour section of Google Analytics, specifically looking at the Site Content > All Pages > Landing pages section as shown in Fig. 12.8.

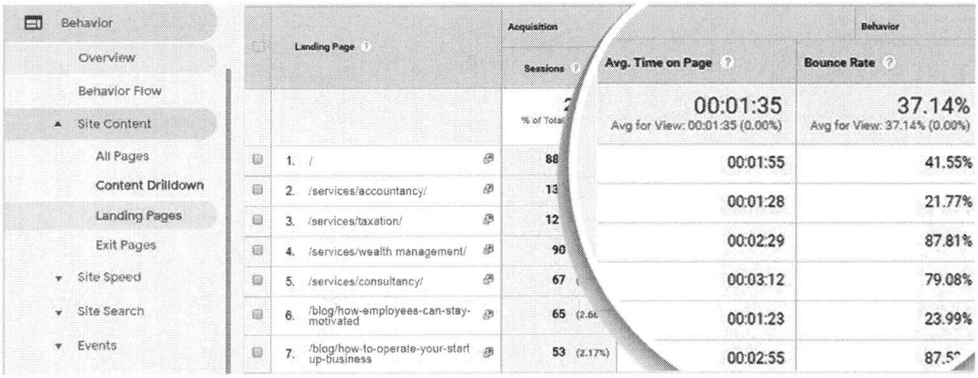

Figure 12.8

Look through every page URL that is listed here, and note what pages are performing and which are flopping. Then, it's up to you to find the solution as to why a page might not be doing as well as expected. You may need to carry out some A/B split testing here. A/B testing is useful for working out which version works best; however, it's a relatively advanced concept, so I'd recommend pressing on with your 'A' draft before working on a 'B' draft to swap in.

Social Media ROI

The next metric tells you how well all those vital social media campaigns are doing. You can look at your in-house social media performance through each of the social media sites themselves, but you likely want to know more than what these can tell you in relation to your website's performance. You really want to know whether your social media content is pushing traffic to your website. This will make it easier to assess the return on investment generated from each social media platform and campaign.

Head on over to the Acquisition section of Google Analytics, then click into Social > Network Referrals, shown in Fig. 12.9. This will tell you how much traffic your website is drawing in from each social media platform.

Figure 12.9

Here you can see that Facebook and LinkedIn seem to be the top two social network platforms driving the most traffic to my client's website.

To help you assess the social media ROI, find out more from the Overview section within Social, as this shows you how much revenue each social media traffic source is earning you. Do this via Acquisition > Social > Overview as in Fig. 12.10. If you invested heavily into video marketing on YouTube but you are seeing poor results, where it's not routing viewers to your website, you have to work out why that is.

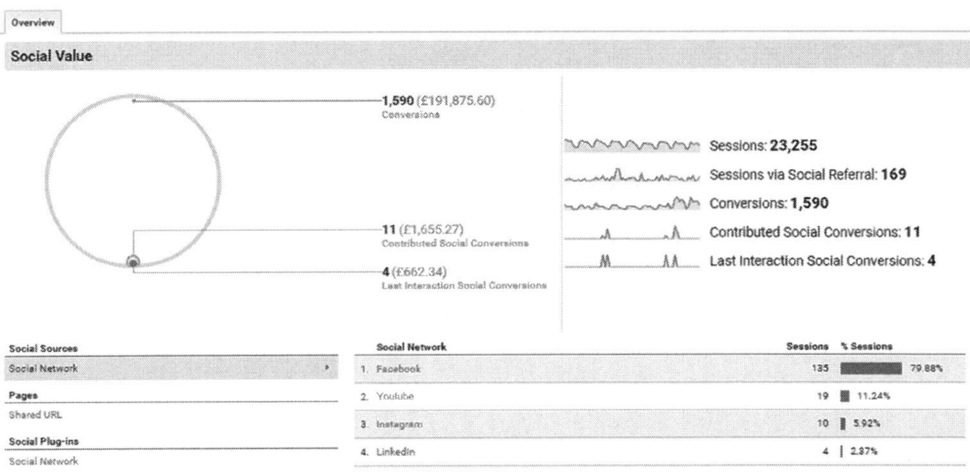

Figure 12.10

If you want to learn a bit more about your social media developments though, you need to use more than Google. Try the very useful Buzzsumo tool seen in Fig. 12.11. This allows you to check out the number of social media shares on a particular page. Check each blog page URL that your business has, and you can find out where your results are coming from. Again, this lets you know what is working and what isn't. Just type in your domain, and you will see the top shared pages of your website from across all the social media sites, as well as your total shares. Knowing this helps you to refine and improve your social media campaigns based on which ones are giving you the highest return on investment.

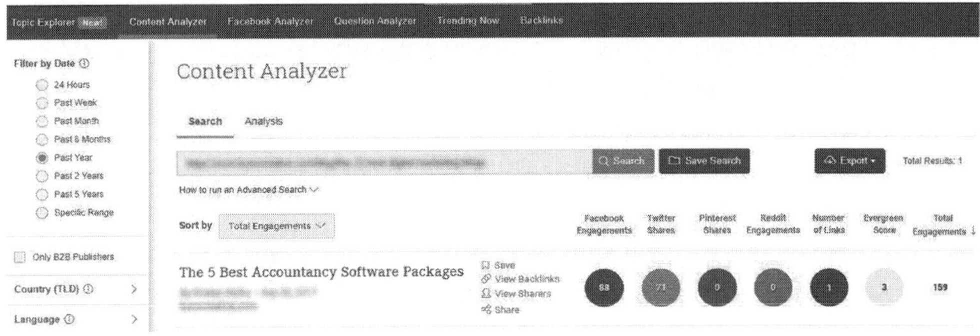

Figure 12.11

SEO ROI

This brings us to the final metric: I hope you now know a fair bit more about SEO than you did previously, but just remember the signs of healthy SEO include:

- ✓ High natural ranking within the search engines for your main keywords.
- ✓ Your domain is appearing with a higher authority thanks to those high-quality backlinks.
- ✓ You are seeing more inbound links coming to your website.

If all this is happening, then you are doing SEO right. How do you know, though?

One way to test if you are doing well could be to go to your preferred web browser and then open up an Incognito/Private browsing session. Search for one of your primary keywords – let's say something simple like 'accountant LOCATION' or 'accountants in LOCATION' – where are you appearing in the search results?

If you are in the top 5, you are doing OK. Top 3, and you can be very satisfied with all your efforts. The top 3 spots garner the lion's share of traffic, with around a third of all traffic going to number 1, and numbers 2 and 3 attracting another 30% between them. The top 5 positions take up just about 70% of the entire search engine spoils!

If you want to know more about your site, then head on over to the Open Site Explorer by Moz. This is also another very handy metrics tool which will give you new measures around your page and overall domain authority, making it easy to get a good idea of how much sway you presently hold. It's another great way to study your inbound links and see who is linking to you. You could even be a little sneaky here and check out your competitors, as I mentioned in Chapter 7.

Improving this can take time, but it's going to be something you need to work at slowly. Remember, optimising your site can take a long time: this won't happen overnight. So long as you are seeing gradual improvements in your metrics, you are on the right track.

Takeaways

- Being able to analyse everything your business is doing now, and in which direction your marketing is leading it, is vital to its long-term prosperity. Without analysis you can't show any success as evidenced by the numbers, otherwise it's hard to know if your digital marketing campaigns are meeting your objectives. And worth the investment of your time and money.
- Your key performance indicators, such as sales, cost per lead, conversion rate and customer lifetime value will be helpful in determining your progress. These are important but also need to work alongside other key metrics.
- From website traffic to lead quality as well as website engagement, you have several metrics to measure using Google Analytics. These will help you to build a more reputable website, in turn generating more leads and bringing in more business.
- Other important elements such as SEO, social media ROI and your Pay-Per-Click ads will all play their part in enhancing your digital marketing strategy. Tracking and measuring the success rate of these metrics will be critical to developing a highly visible and advantageous online presence for your business.

JUST ONE MORE THING...

"The path to success is to take massive, determined actions" – Tony Robbins

Now you've read through my book and hopefully found it useful, I dare say you're ready to take action and put it all into practice. You may have a few ideas racing around in your head, and likely feeling eager to get started with implementing these marketing strategies to reel in those big fish clients. If that's the case – great! My job here is done. I'm confident that with the tools and techniques you've learned, you'll be in a much better position to start growing your business and attracting your ideal clients. I'm also positive that, in time, you'll attract more than you can cope with. Isn't that a nice position to be in, to choose who you take on?

Just let me know how you get on with your results. I'd love to hear how your firm grows in the years to come.

However, I also figure that – for some sections at least – you might be feeling a little overwhelmed. Or concerned you won't have the time to implement these marketing tactics and/or social media campaigns while running your business. You won't be the first, nor the last, in that position, and perhaps would prefer some assistance to put everything in place – that's also fine.

Remember, the key is to take action, whether you do it yourself or decide to hire an expert to do it for you. If you'd like some professional help then my team at Marketing for Professionals are more than happy to set you up with the right marketing campaign, improve your current ones or anything else.

If you'd like to discuss this further, please get in touch via email at:

info@marketingforprofessionals.co.uk

For those of you who would like to hire me personally to:

- Run workshops on LinkedIn for you and your staff
- Teach you more advanced marketing strategies

- Review your current marketing activities and campaigns
- Review your business goals and provide you with a clear strategic focus
- Attend a 3 day course on internet marketing
- Benefit from my 1:1 strategic consulting

You can email me at:

nick@thesmestrategist.com

Mandeep Ubhi FCCA – (Director, Morgan Reach)

Nick helped me formulate a comprehensive marketing plan specifically for LinkedIn. This included some excellent tools to address the challenge of measuring the impact of the campaign. I liaise regularly with Nick as part of his consulting package – a valuable resource that ensures the highest level of efficiency. He also holds you accountable for your actions moving forward and expands your knowledge and understanding of digital marketing strategy. His professional guidance and expertise are always appreciated.

Vincent Tong – (Consultant Solicitor, Head of Immigration, Valens Solicitors)

Nick and I met at a London networking event. My marketing needs were complex, and I was seeking a bespoke solution. I needed an expert who not only understood the specific marketing resources I required, but who could take the initiative when necessary. Nick met these demands and has become a valuable contact. He is highly professional and reliable. I have no hesitation in recommending his services.

Victoria Jane – (Online Business Manager and Virtual Assistant Coach, Victoria Jane Assists)

Nick's practical and strategic advice has been incredibly useful to me and my business. I get to sit down with Nick on a quarterly basis to discuss my business results. I've used a few consultants in the past but nothing quite like what Nick offers. Not only does he provide tremendous value, he helps motivate me to ensure my plans come to fruition.

About the Author

Dubbed 'The SME Strategist' by the Internet Business School and Business Growth School, NICK BAGGA is the founder of Marketing for Professionals, a digital marketing company specialising in helping professional service firms increase their visibility, attract more leads and boost bottom line profits.

A former accountant turned digital marketing consultant, Nick helps and advises SMEs on implementing the most effective digital marketing strategies for their circumstances. Bringing together expertise in both finance and marketing, Nick shows his clients how to improve their online position, while helping them focus on the small changes they can make that yield big outcomes for their business.

Prior to launching Marketing for Professionals, Nick worked for large corporates where he operated on multi-million pound projects and led a team of developers to create high value, cutting edge, cloud-based solutions for SMEs across the UK. While he enjoyed this role, Nick found his true calling in assisting smaller businesses to evolve their own unique brand, empowering them to grow beyond their existing means.

His real passion lies in strategic marketing, fusing together his knowledge of corporate finance and networking to help others generate high returns on investment. With an intuitive understanding of what professionals want to say and what potential clients want to hear, he blends a 'best of both worlds' approach to marketing. This provides significant value to businesses and individuals, tailoring digital marketing to their own personal needs, aims and objectives.

Nick believes that by embracing the digital age professionals and others can harness technology to improve not only their personal brand, but also their work-life balance. He champions a freedom-based lifestyle, without corporate restrictions, combining both business and pleasure as he advises clients around the world. He gains great satisfaction from coaching, consulting and training others so they can achieve their ambitions and see their dreams become reality.

Connect with Nick

https://www.linkedin.com/in/nickbagga/

Contact Nick

nick@thesmestrategist.com

nick@marketingforprofessionals.co.uk

I value your opinion. Please tell me what you think.

I hope you found this book valuable.

My overall aim was to help you understand digital marketing in more detail and make informed choices when it comes to applying that knowledge.

If you feel the book has achieved that goal (or not) then I'd really value some feedback. You can email me at: nick@thesmestrategist.com

Alternatively, you can write an Amazon review – I read them all, so any feedback on good points and what needs improving will help me with future editions.

Thanks for reading my book and I wish you every success with your marketing efforts.

Nick